Peter Fisher is a priest of the Church in the Diocese of Birmingham. Brc he studied in Durham and has w Sunderland and Birmingham. His ministry has been divided between parish work in the north and the Midlands, and theological education (he was at one time Sub-Warden of Lincoln Theological College and, more recently, Principal of the Queen's Foundation, Birmingham). His teaching experience is in systematic theology, and he is deeply involved in ecumenical work and writing. Elizabeth, his wife, is a New Testament specialist who is also active in the ecumenical movement.

OUTSIDE EDEN

Finding hope in an imperfect world

Peter Fisher

First published in Great Britain in 2009

Society for Promoting Christian Knowledge
36 Causton Street
London SW1P 4ST

British Library Cataloguing-in-Publication Data
A catalogue record for this book is available from the British Library

ISBN 978–0–281–05995–9

1 3 5 7 9 10 8 6 4 2

Typeset by Graphicraft Ltd, Hong Kong
Printed in Great Britain by Ashford Colour Press

Produced on paper from sustainable forests

To Elizabeth
who has been and is to me
like the 'fixt foot' of John Donne's twin compasses
whose 'firmness makes my circle just
and makes me end, where I begunne'
(John Donne, 'A Valediction: Forbidding Mourning')

I am bound to continue to get love wrong, all the time,
but never to cease loving, for this is my life's affair, love's work
Gillian Rose, *Love's Work*

Contents

Foreword

It was a great spiritual guide of the early twentieth century who said that, while innocence might have been the best thing for Adam in the Garden of Eden, the best thing for us fallen human beings was forgiveness. Something like this insight is at the heart of Peter Fisher's humane and wise reflections. Facing our unfinishedness, our imperfect humanity – which is the only sort of humanity we can experience – should not be frightening or humiliating; simply a matter of hard but life-giving truthfulness. Confronting the mature fullness of humanity in Jesus Christ is not gazing resentfully at an ideal we can never achieve, but encountering an unending resource of promise – a relationship that we shall never exhaust, in the context of which we can grow with and through our failings.

Peter Fisher puts his finger with deadly accuracy on a couple of major errors we can fall into when we try to understand all this. When we're delivered from the prison of perfectionism, we can lock ourselves into another kind of prison where we pretend that there is nothing the matter after all ('I'm OK, you're OK'). It's a prison because it's static and because it's a way of denying loss and real frustration and honest awareness of the damage we do to others and ourselves. Reach too quickly for the language of inclusiveness and acceptance, and you leave no room for transformation; you end up expecting less of yourself and your world than you might.

There is a tightrope to walk between obsessive perfectionism and apathetic acceptance. Somewhere between them lies the acceptance that is both truthful and hopeful: 'This is what I am and it is not all that I hope to be; may I let God in to what I truly am now, so that he may lead me to places I don't yet know.'

Woven through this book is the work of one of the twentieth century's greatest English poets, W. H. Auden. Peter rightly sees him as speaking for just this kind of mixture of honesty and hope, and uses to great effect Auden's wry, sad, witty and deeply affirming voice to provide a sort of echo chamber for his own meditations. It is a deeply moving combination.

Foreword

Written with clarity and personal candour, repeatedly stepping back to ask whether he's made it too easy or failed to sustain the balance, Peter's book is a gently probing, compassionate invitation to learn how to live in an unfinished humanity, in the presence of grace, maintained in truth, animated by mercy and hope.

+Rowan Cantuar:
Lambeth Palace

Preface and acknowledgements

Writing a book, if this one is anything to go by, offers just one uncomplicated pleasure: that of expressing thanks to those who have helped – or, at least, to some of them.

Friends have played a large part. The first spur to get down to writing came, with characteristic firmness, from Caroline Dick. Early encouragement was given by Michael Kitchener and by Nicola Slee, whose gift for combining affirmation and critique was invaluable later, too. I also owe a special debt to Rachel Webbley, who was so generous as to read most of the text as it emerged, attending sympathetically to what I was trying to say and commenting perceptively. In so far as the finished book makes sense, this owes a great deal to her acute and helpful interrogation of the text. At difficult junctures in the writing, conversations with David Scott and my son, David Fisher, were a great help. Kenneth Wilson has lent support and Brother Anselm SSF has kept watch over the project all the way through.

The time to write was allowed me by the generosity of the Parish of St Peter's, Maney, with the unstinting support and help of Mark Pryce and Bishop David Urquhart, and also of Philip Swan.

I hope that my debts of gratitude to writers, past and present, are apparent from the book itself. Providence was kind in leading me to take W. H. Auden's poetry as a source of inspiration and stimulation; my appreciation of his work has been enhanced by frequent reference to Humphrey Carpenter's biography of the poet.

The staff of SPCK Publishers has been all that an inexperienced author could wish for. I am particularly appreciative of the detailed attention, help and guidance given by Rebecca Mulhearn, my editor, from the time she first took an interest in the infant proposal to its completion.

By his own example, as well as his writing, Archbishop Rowan Williams had already made a profound contribution to this little book long before he did it the honour of writing the Foreword. Now I offer heartfelt thanks for both these contributions.

Pride of place in these words of thanks belongs to Elizabeth, my wife. The book is dedicated to her, and justly so, not only for all the big things that make her a wonderful person to be married to, but for the loving attention to detail that she has given, all the way along, to this text.

The imperfections that remain, I can say with an absolutely straight face, are entirely my responsibility!

Introduction: well outside Eden

This book is about *imperfection* and about how we respond to imperfection. It is a subject we all know something about, but not a subject that can be tackled entirely in the abstract. Ideals, perhaps, may be sketched out in general, but imperfection belongs in the realm of particular reality, of experience. So this kind of exploration has to be rooted in personal experience. But whose personal experience? Only a satirist or a writer of political propaganda can get away with showing up the flaws of others while concealing their own (or should we include some journalists, too?). So, although this is not a book about me, it has to be candid about me, the author.

In fact this book aims to be about something exponentially greater than any of us – about love of a kind that tangles with human imperfection, embraces it and blesses it. That love is the heart of the gospel (and by gospel I mean not just the words written down in the four Gospels, but the whole gift of a new way of seeing and being that is given in Jesus Christ). But to understand and feel how this love – the love of God – takes hold of us in our imperfection we need to attend to our own, very specific stories, with their own specific mishaps, successes, jokes and tragedies. Without that attention, redemption remains a theory.

'To generalize', wrote William Blake in one of his more trenchant moments, 'is to be an idiot. To particularize is the Alone Distinction of Merit.'[1] And with more than a nod in his direction, writing this book I have tried to keep checking what I write against the particulars of my own experience.

But, be reassured, this is not really a *confessional* book. The writing of confessions is best left to genuine saints or truly eye-popping sinners. I will come clean about my experiences – some of them, at least – as this book unfolds. But these experiences of mine are only one voice in a conversation that makes up this book. I have only come to know about myself – a little bit, at least – through the companionship and love, the conversation and questioning of others. So, in the same way, I can only explore and write about the shared human experience of imperfection through a kind of companionable conversation. In this book I have chosen several poets as companions. First among them is W. H. Auden, who was born a hundred years ago and died in 1973. The companionship he offers here is through his living voice, his writings. Early on in life he realized that he wanted – or *had* – to be a poet. When he died he left a legacy of hundreds of poems and some important prose works.[2] At least one of the poems ('Stop All the Clocks',[3] read out in church at the funeral in the film *Four Weddings and a Funeral*) is well known. More of them are being appreciated now, as his life and work come to be seen in their true stature.

There are two main reasons why Auden is a good companion in this journey of exploration. The first is because after he found (or rediscovered) it around the age of 31, faith was a deep and pervasive influence on his writing, even though believing was never straightforward for him and was always accompanied by a dose of scepticism. The second is that all his work bears the mark of someone who kept his feet very firmly on the ground – hence the mixture of faith and scepticism. The depth and intelligence of his reading and thinking about Christian faith made him, nonetheless, a genuine if somewhat maverick theologian. He was well able to quote Augustine from the fifth century or Paul Tillich from the twentieth. But his expression of theology was not only humane and generous-spirited, it was also unequivocally *human*. Auden's poetry is, if you like, always about imperfection, though it is about a great deal more than that, as we shall see. He has helped me to recognize where I am – well and truly outside Eden, the place of perfection, but also *well* outside Eden; not always happy to be imperfect, but rejoicing.

1

Recognizing where we are: facing up to imperfection

Auden provides my starting point in one of his earlier ballad-like poems, 'As I Walked Out One Evening'. Early on in the poem we hear an extravagant declaration of eternal love ('I'll love you, dear, I'll love you / Till China and Africa meet . . .'). Then this declaration of love is confronted by the inexorable chiming of the clock ('Time watches from the shadow / And coughs when you would kiss.'). The dream of undying love is cruelly undermined. So where will the poem go from here? We might think that, like Andrew Marvell's wonderful exercise in joyful cynicism, 'To his Coy Mistress', it will develop into a plea to 'make hay while the sun shines' and enjoy love while it lasts. Or it might prove to be a sad reflection on the transience of everything lovely on earth. In Auden's hands, however, it turns out quite unexpectedly. Here are the last three verses:

'O look, look in the mirror,
O look in your distress;
Life remains a blessing
Although you cannot bless.

'O stand, stand at the window
As the tears scald and start;
You shall love your crooked neighbour
With your crooked heart.'

It was late, late in the evening,
The lovers, they were gone;
The clocks had ceased their chiming,
And the deep river ran on.

'You shall love your crooked neighbour / With your crooked heart'! This is what follows after disillusion. When I have looked in the mirror, and seen the worst that it has to show me, when I have stared

1

through the window and been horrified by what I see in the world beyond, I end up encountering this most unexpected command, backed up by an equally unexpected assurance: 'Life remains a blessing / Although you cannot bless.'

Those arresting and puzzling verses, written in the run-up to World War Two,[1] and at the point when Auden was hovering on the brink of commitment to Christian faith, sum up the trajectory of this book: how reflection on being an imperfect creature in an imperfect, time-bound world can lead to hope, faith and even love.

'O look, look in the mirror.' When I look in the mirror, on most occasions the mirror gives back to me what I expect. A mechanical glance – combing my hair or washing – simply confirms the image of my face that I keep on file, somewhere in the cabinet of my consciousness. This is not an image that shocks or specially disturbs me. If I am upset to see shadows under the eyes or more pronounced furrows on the brow this is more like a concern for what is happening to me as time passes, rather than concern about 'who I am'. I am, in fact, rather comfortable with this familiar image. Of course I can acknowledge that this is not the most handsome or even youthful of faces. But such 'modesty' does little to undermine my pervasively comfortable feeling. Like other forms of self-deprecation, this awareness of my own imperfections always assumes a friendly rejoinder: 'Oh no, you don't look that age at all!' On the whole, my imagination, like a flattering portrait painter, depicts me in a kindly light.

When I consider the command of Jesus to 'love my neighbour *as myself*', I believe it relates to this 'default setting' or underlying presumption that I hold, inwardly, about myself. The way I love myself is deep-seated and automatic; the self-critical attitudes that are included in this self-love are a bit like the sarcastic comments we exchange with a most trusted friend: they prove how much at home we are with one another. Strangely, I can even carry on loving myself in this way when I am furiously annoyed or deeply ashamed about myself. To love someone *else* – let alone every neighbour – in such a way takes some imagining.

To return to my mirror, however: just occasionally it gives me back something I was not looking for. I remember staying three nights in a strange house. In the bathroom was a huge floor-to-ceiling mirror. There was no avoiding it. The effect of walking in front of it was as unsettling as suddenly hearing your own voice played back by a tape or CD recorder. No, it was worse, because it had the brutal immediacy of sight. This cannot be me! It was not an image I felt at home with or even wanted to acknowledge as my own. It was the wrong shape; it had characteristics I simply did not like. After this, to go on a diet was only a superficial response to what I had been forced to see: a me who seemed – well, ugly.

These two kinds of mirror image – one that fits my residual self-awareness and one that assails and unsettles it – begin to open up my understanding of imperfection. First there is a kind of acceptable, or benign, imperfection. If we were to agree an abstract definition of 'the perfect face', or even to picture a face that looks perfect to me and you, you could easily point out the ways in which my own face falls short; but I would probably keep smiling while you told me.

There are many ways in which imperfection – if that means falling short of an abstract ideal, or a dream of what is perfect – is acceptable, or has gradually become acceptable, to most of us. We may look back, wryly, on the struggles of late childhood and adolescence, when we were agonizingly 'coming to terms with' our limitations, with bad skin, unglamorous hair, a mathematically challenged brain or failure to attract devotees. But to be adult, to have 'put away childish things', means, among other things, to come to a settlement of some kind, a form of acceptance of our personal limitations and deficiencies. This acceptance may be exposed as fragile at times, should I fall into despair or depression about myself. And it can equally be *too ready* an acceptance, allowing us to live too lazily at ease with inadequacies we condemn in other people. But for all this, life teaches us to negotiate quite peacefully with much that we might, theoretically, wish to be otherwise.

Reflecting on imperfection may take us further than this, so far as to raise the question whether we can in fact tolerate perfection. I don't mean 'tolerate' just in relation to the annoyance, the intolerance, most of us feel when someone is 'always right', when she or he knows – and tells you – the right answer to every question, or when someone smiles on you with graceful condescension, displaying perfect teeth. That intolerance is the product, mostly, of chagrin or jealousy.

At a deeper level, however, it is not only hard to know what a perfect world would be like, but also whether we could survive it.

Clearly, if perfection is understood to mean 'lacking *any* limitation', then it is quite beyond our imagining. In truth, it can only properly be ascribed to God. We can only 'comprehend' or 'get our heads around' things that are in some way defined and distinct: we can see *this* because it is not *that*.

But perhaps we can have a more modest definition of what is perfect. We could try 'lacking any defect'. We would mean by that, 'not lacking anything that (it/she/he) should have'. This is more like the way we usually use the word perfect, in practice. When we look back on a 'perfect holiday' we mean that it had everything a holiday should have. It was probably spent in good company, with relaxation, sunshine, good mattresses . . . Or was it? The family cynic, when the photographs of this 'perfect' holiday are being passed round, will refer to the cockroaches in the bedroom, the three days of incessant rain and the moment when you realized that you were driving in the wrong direction up a continental motorway. Yet you insist that it was perfect, or perhaps say that you 'wouldn't have changed a thing about it'. And perhaps the cynic and you are both right. Yes, it rained, but that was why the family sat down and talked, and how we needed to talk! Yes, there were cockroaches, but the *patron* was mortified and moved us to the room with a balcony. In other words what we, commonly speaking, mean by perfection has a way of including imperfections.

The same can be said of our perception of beauty, or at least of more complex and subtle forms of beauty. If we confine our attention to objects with only one or two dimensions or those that are products of design and artifice – as when we look at a picture, hear music, or look at a sculpture or a viaduct – we may be able to say, 'That is perfect', meaning precisely that it is lacking any defect, at least in our own judgement. Hard though it is to pin down the criteria, or standards of judgement that we use to tell whether the image of a face or a song has everything an image of a face or a song should have, at least we can have a stab, using words like balance, shape, proportion. These criteria may not, of course, help us discern what constitutes a great work of art, which we often speak of as having 'something indefinable' about it.[2] The point is not that we have a complete or very robust definition of what we mean by 'beautiful' in these cases, but that we use the word, in these instances, to mean something like 'lacking any defect'.

However, as soon as we introduce further dimensions or take away the limits that frame a performance, an icon or a man-made structure, we find that our view of beauty has subtly changed. It is different in two ways. One has to do with sheer complexity: when it is a landscape or a life that we are looking at there are an incalculable number and range of factors contributing to the judgement, 'That is beautiful'. The attempt to justify our judgement by any general criteria becomes ridiculous; we can only say, 'Can't you see?' But the other difference is more interesting. When we call a landscape or a life beautiful, we know that it can only have that quality by *including* defects: the canker on the trees, the parched grass; or the loss of a first child, the inability to sing in tune, or to thread a needle. Such things, each of which taken alone appears as a moral or visual blot on the landscape, become integral parts of the beauty of the whole scene.

This 'embracing' of defects in beauty ties in with the fact that our perception of beauty is closely allied to affection and love. Nowhere is this clearer than at the time of a funeral. Before the service, members of the family (the 'next of kin', a phrase that emerges only at this painful juncture) speak to the priest about the person who has died. Where relationships with that person have been awkward, the picture that emerges will be either of someone faultless or of someone with a long catalogue of failings. Where the relationships have been loving, there will almost always tumble out a captivating succession of images and stories that illuminate how precious this person's life was and is; and the anecdotes that will provoke tears are those that tell of her or his failings, weaknesses and 'bad habits' – as if these were the very focal points of love. Robin Williams, playing the part of a somewhat unorthodox psychiatrist in the film *Good Will Hunting* makes the same point in a sentimental but powerful way: 'No, that's the real stuff, it's all those little peculiarities and defects; they're what you treasure most when you love someone.'[3] Looking back, when we try to sum up the 'beauty' of a life, the imperfections contribute something vital.

The Christian tradition affirms that the risen and ascended Christ still bears in his body the nail-marks from his crucifixion. Thank God for that. If there were no heavenly equivalent to the scars, creases and defects that mark our lives, we would no longer recognize, nor, perhaps, be able to love one another there. Somehow, the Christian vision of glory has to incorporate, in Charles Wesley's words, 'glorious scars'.[4]

None of this amounts to saying that imperfection is somehow 'a good thing' in itself; to say so would be to twist language. But it does mean recognizing how inextricably imperfection is bound up in our experience of the world and how far – with or without faith – we may at times be able to see our world as, strangely, the richer for it.

However, there are many manifestations of imperfection that can be neither calmly accepted nor fitted into any satisfactory big picture. Indeed, the same defect that seems charming from one perspective may be viciously malign from another viewpoint. Murderers often seem like good neighbours to those close, but not too close, to them. Part of the significance of living in an imperfect world lies in the reality of chance and unreliability, whereby something in itself quite trivial can cause mayhem. Another part lies in the presence of things (including human characteristics) that are of their very nature dangerous and destructive. To describe evil as a form of 'imperfection' does not diminish its malevolence, still less make it acceptable. Life forces on our attention aspects of ourselves and our world that are outrageous. Most often we experience outrage at a distance, waxing indignant at our TV screens or at the driver in the car in front; but traumatic events bring the realization closer to home. Earlier I was describing the shock of seeing myself in a full-length mirror. But this is only a two-dimensional shock. A whole extra dimension of pain and confusion comes when it is rejection by other people (or another, important, person), or patent breakdown in our work or home that confronts us. To see myself as unlovely, or ugly, is one thing. To encounter the brute fact of other people's distrust or enmity, that they see and treat me as ugly, is quite another. This we cannot bear – the kind of trauma that comes through the violence of or rejection by others, or my own naked failure – or can bear only with generous help and the painful passage of time.

In a similar way, we may be troubled by a good documentary programme about HIV/Aids in the developing world. More than that, to see the reality of it for ourselves, as visitors, or because the same disease has touched our family, will redouble the impact. But perhaps it is only those who themselves share, or have shared, the experience of life-threatening sickness who can acknowledge just what this kind of 'imperfection' means. The throw-away phrase, 'Well, none of us is perfect', does not begin to touch the experiences of real harm that we undergo – and inflict. Nor does it begin to do justice to the excess of deprivation, impairment and pain that is suffered in the local psychiatric ward, the shacks of Zimbabwe or, perhaps, the kitchen or bedroom next door.

Soon after writing 'As I Walked Out One Evening', Auden was caught up in the beginnings of the war. Already widely known as a poet, his decision in 1939 to move to the United States was openly criticized as a betrayal of his nation. In spite of his previous commitment to pacifism, he tried to offer his services to his country in any way that might be of value. The offer was declined, on account, it seems, of his homosexuality. Something more personally bitter was to follow. A couple of years after Auden had emigrated, the man he loved, Chester Kallman, admitted to being unfaithful to him. This was a shattering blow. Auden had not only fallen in love with Kallman but had come to think of the relationship as a marriage, a relationship of lifelong, undivided commitment, and he believed that fidelity in homosexual relationships was specially important.[5] Could he still assert that 'life remains a blessing', in the light of the malevolent horror of the Third Reich and the war, and in the blighting of his personal life too? Whether he looked in the mirror or through the window, the prospects for loving his neighbour, even with a 'crooked' love, did not seem promising.

Yet Auden's new-found faith, and the rugged streak of hopefulness in his character that went with it, held through these trials. More than that, it seems to have matured. The autumn of 1941 finds him writing 'A Christmas Oratorio' (entitled *For the Time Being*), an extended work in which his personal faith was more explicit than ever before. And here, the wise men at the manger sing, 'The choice to love is open till we die', and the shepherds sing to the infant Christ:

> O Living Love, by your birth we are able
> Not only, like the ox and ass of the stable,
> To love with our live wills, but love,
> Knowing we love.

And knowing – he might well have added, had it been another sort of poem – the kind of world love is up against and the kind of impaired hearts, minds and capacities that have to do the loving.

The circumstances of my own life, almost all of them, are quite different from those of Auden's. Many details of his personal belief, if I understand them rightly, are different from mine; some seem to me odd. Yet he can articulate, in a distinct and memorable voice, the common themes that animate this book, themes that are as dear to me as I believe they were to him. And, because of his uncompromising honesty, he can help to anchor this exploration in realism, as well as in faith.

For my hope is this: to show how faith can make its home in this world, *my* world of imperfection, how it can root, grow and flower here. As such, this exploration is a bit unusual, even odd. It might seem, at times, like a study of 'the problem of evil' or an investigation of 'sin' and 'forgiveness'. But it is not quite any of these things. The difference is partly to do with trying to avoid terms like sin and evil, which bear a heavy weight of traditional interpretation. It has more to do, though, with something positive, something perhaps best expressed in the words of another poem, this time by Edwin Muir: 'One Foot in Eden'. The poem depicts our world as a landscape darkened by evil, a land quite unlike the garden of Eden, a land in which weeds and corn grow inseparably intertwined. Yet in the end it is not so bleak a vision:

> . . . famished field and blackened tree
> Bear flowers in Eden never known.
> Blossoms of grief and charity
> Bloom in these darkened fields alone.
> What had Eden ever to say
> Of hope and faith and pity and love
> Until was buried all its day
> And memory found its treasure trove?
> Strange blessings never in Paradise
> Fall from these beclouded skies.

This, then, is a study of the 'strange blessings' that are the fruits of the gospel – good news which is particularly addressed to this peculiar, impaired world. I hope to trace the intriguing symbiosis between the grace of God, as Jesus brings it to us, and our real, imperfect lives, in the belief that it leads, not perhaps to perfection, but to glory.

*   *   *

On further reflection . . .

Perhaps, like me, you are wondering what sort of person would write a book about imperfection. Might it be someone with a bit of a penchant for compromise, settling for second best? Someone not quite brave enough to aim for real holiness of life? It could be someone who wants to have his cake and eat it, to pray (as St Augustine wrote of his former self), 'Lord, make me pure – but not yet.' It isn't easy, is it, to know when acceptance of weakness is the fruit of honesty and faith, and when it is a bit of a cop-out?

2

Loving our mess: the gospel and human unsuccess

I ruined my own eighth birthday party. It was a big party, in spite of the residual austerity of the 1950s. My parents must have made a special effort. After 'tea', the living-room carpet was rolled back and we all played a rather rumbustious game which I then knew as 'British Bulldog'. As I remember, it involved all of us children hopping about (literally) with arms folded and attempting to knock one another over – rather like dodgem cars at the fairground. In this particular game it became progressively clear that all the other children were ganging up to knock over my best friend. Anger welled up in me until something in me broke: furious, I stood (on both feet) in the middle of the room and bellowed out, 'Bloody, bloody, bloody!' I'm not sure exactly what happened next, but I know there was no more party.

> Beloved, we are always in the wrong,
> Handling so clumsily our stupid lives . . .

So wrote Auden in his great poem of love (and war) 'In Sickness and in Health'. Starting the verse with the warm word, 'Beloved', as he does, affects the mood of the poet's statement. We hear it not so much as a bitter, angry or despairing cry but as a wry, companionable and almost philosophical admission, perhaps just tinged with exasperation. It is the way we often feel when looking back on our lives. The words were written in the year 1940 – 'a murderous year', as Auden called it. This was a time when it was impossible to ignore the destructive energies and 'howling appetites' of human beings. Yet the poem remains fundamentally a poem of love. It is an exercise in bringing love face to face with harsh reality, the reality of 'How warped [are] the mirrors where our worlds are made'. The reason why our human love can face this reality is because we hear a voice that calls, commands and encourages us. In prose we might call this the voice of God, and it is clear that this is what Auden believes it is. But he calls it 'Love's peremptory word' – a phrase rich in association, when we remember that John's Gospel calls Christ the 'Word made flesh'. The voice calls to us from amid the chaos of life (the *tohu-bohu*, Auden calls it, echoing the Hebrew words from Genesis 1.2, 'a formless void'), and commands us to 'rejoice'.

It is not enough, of course, to be *told* to rejoice. And in this poem there is something else, something surprising. The God who commands us is the Creator, but not just the Creator as usually understood. This Creator has a 'talent for the makeshift', for making life and beauty out of 'odds and ends'. In a flash we can see the vision that Auden is summoning to our imagination. It is a vision of the world as an astounding yet almost comical miracle, a miracle in which 'savage elements' – physical and emotional – are taught to dance, and the beauty of the one we love is conjured out of chaos. Essentially it is a vision of grace, the absolute opposite of every view that takes for granted the way things are, or gives us credit for having got where we are. Everything, including you and I, says Auden, exists 'by grace of the Absurd'. Why the Absurd? And why with a capital 'A'? Well, the capital tells us that this is a new name for God, and the name is not just a joke, as if God were being ridiculed. Break down the word – Ab-surd – and it implies 'From-chaos' or out of incoherence. The grace of God is always the grace of the 'Absurd', taking the incoherent, broken bits of life and eliciting meaning, shape and purpose from them, rather as a cross was formed of blackened nails in the bombed-out cathedral in Coventry.

The absurdity of grace stands out as a feature of the stories so many people tell about God's calling, or vocation. 'Who would have dreamt', we say, 'that *I* would end up doing this?' Very occasionally, of course, a naturally talented speaker is drawn to a ministry of preaching. But more often, people who feel called to stand up and preach feel, at the same time, that this is the *last* thing they are cut out to do. There is a sensation, common to people who respond to some kind of calling, of walking the high wire and being amazed that this is me doing it. Surely this is true not only of obviously vocational people, like clergy, but of all who sense that they are called and empowered to step out in a new and unselfish direction. It can certainly be true of someone who, having fallen in love, finds an answering love bounding back to meet them. Such people find themselves unaccountably singing or laughing as they walk along the street. In all these circumstances there is a joyful incongruity, a sense of the absurd and of the glory of what is undeserved.

Time, now, to recall my eighth birthday, when the party ended. Occasions such as this stick in the mind: but not only as scars or 'unhappy memories'. When the inner tingle of embarrassment has died away (which may take a decade or more) we begin dimly to make out something else; how this moment, and similar moments of outrage and breakdown, may have been formative. There are, of course, two things that can go wrong after a disaster. One is that it is rapidly followed by another, and another: the parents thrash the foul-mouthed child, the child steals from the parents, the parents disown the child . . . The other is quite the opposite: the disaster is ignored, covered up or quickly smothered with cuddles and consolation before there is any chance to recognize and accept what has gone wrong. The second course of action is less blatantly damaging, but repeated over time it saps the ability of both parent and child to face difficult realities, and so encourages the festering rather than the healing of sores.

There is, however, a third option, which takes time to work its way through and which may go unperceived. The parents might be brave enough to hold off from the temptation either to punish or to protect their child. They might not know what exactly to say or do beyond admitting the fact that things have gone awry and that a bit of chaos has broken in to cause multiple little ripples of hurt and shame. Allowing this *time* might mean that the child begins to recognize chaos and hurt; without realizing it the child may begin to sense that even disaster does not have to be fled or instantly escaped. It could also be a time for recognition of the factors and forces at work in this chaos – both within and outside the child – and the emergence of a sense of responsibility in which he neither denies all blame nor thrusts it all on to others.

Who knows whether punishment might follow? By this time it might no longer seem necessary. Because, finally, the love that made the parents brave enough to wait and the child brave enough to ponder will begin a work that is more than healing. This work will include 'drawing a line' under what happened – and strangely, this line, which is a mark of forgiveness, an indication that blame and guilt will not be carried forward from this point, in fact *allows* the event to become creative and energizing for the future. Once this line is drawn (and it must be indelibly drawn) the event can subtly and gradually become a family joke. Told in the right way, the joke is a precious memento of breakage and repair within the family, a way of sustaining the family's shared awareness that chaos may be overcome. That's why family jokes so often focus on disaster. But the joke is not the only survival from that day. There is, too, an unspoken but profound new awareness of both fragility and strength: the fragility of our good selves, and the undreamt-of strength of the bonds of love.

Relationships with such a history behind them have special durability. Nicola Slee, the writer and poet, saw this quality in a sculpture of the Visitation (Mary meeting with Elizabeth) high up in Chartres Cathedral:

> Fragile, yet there is power in the grip of these hands.
> They will not let go.
> Forged for ever in time
> only tenderness could stand so firm.[1]

One moment of disaster, then, might spark a tiny realization of chaos and of grace: tiny, but powerful. And it might be a trivial but real clue to the way the gospel encounters our imperfection.

*   *   *

It may seem grandiose – indeed it is – but I want to compare this aspect of my life story to a Mozart piano concerto. The concerto begins with uncomplicated élan: the orchestra states a confident theme in the major key and soon the piano is limpidly and cheerfully echoing the theme, varying and developing it in a comfortable conversation with the strings and woodwind. Up to this point, the Mozart concerto is much like the works of other composers of his day: graceful and pleasing. But now comes the unexpected. The piano quite abruptly moves to the minor key, announcing a theme that assaults and challenges the mood that has gone before and compelling the orchestra to come along with it. From now on the concerto has a different character. Two things have happened: the confident charm of the opening theme has been exposed as fragile, and at the same time a kind of dynamic, an urgency that pushes the music and the hearer forward, has been unleashed. It is the dynamic of resolution, perhaps eventually of redemption. We listen now with a little yearning inside, a hardly conscious but potent desire to discover that these two incongruous themes, these 'subjects', can be reconciled. The composer has dared to let loose a little bit of chaos: knowing Mozart as we do, we trust his genius to conjure a higher harmony from it. Maynard Solomon has written suggestively about this quality in Mozart's music. He writes about the final bars of the Piano Sonata in C, K.545: 'In the end . . . we have returned to Eden, laden with memories of exile but relieved to have found so felicitous a homecoming.'[2]

It is his ability not only to write music that is colourful, elegant and virtuosic, but also to take this compositional risk that makes Mozart's music so moving. That is, perhaps, also why he is, above all, the composer of *grace*, as the towering twentieth-century theologian Karl Barth knew so well.

In our own lives (as indeed in Mozart's), the introduction of a little chaos is not exactly a choice. We cannot help handling our lives clumsily, and even if we didn't, others would do it for us. So our personal stories – as we remember them – are interspersed with moments of disaster, with times when imperfection bares its teeth.

The singularity of the Christian gospel is that this, however, is its natural soil. In one sense this has always been well known. People who grew up with the Book of Common Prayer ('1662', as it was often known) can probably recite the 'comfortable words' by memory, including the words: 'This is a true saying and worthy of all men to be received, that Christ Jesus came into the world to save sinners' (1 Timothy 1.15). But for many of us, for me at least, those words communicate a certain, limited truth while leaving a wider, more universal awareness dormant. The limited (not unimportant) truth is that Jesus, in his incarnation, his life, his death and his resurrection, reached out, acted and suffered to forgive and restore people who recognized themselves as 'sinners'. And for those (us) sinners who believe in him now, he offers the same forgiveness and restoration. But the wider awareness is this: that, mysteriously, God seems to love a mess, particularly *our* kind of mess.

The picture that springs to my mind is of Theodore Matthieson, an Anglican monk who ran a boys' orphanage in the outskirts of Calcutta. He was a person of indomitable hope and limitless enterprise. I was with him one day when news came that the boys' latrines were blocked. His face lit up, as if on hearing rare and unforeseen good news, and he strode off to deal with the situation with what I can only describe as glee, pulling up the sleeves of his white cassock.

To say this – that God loves a mess – is, of course, to put it crudely. There is a lot more to be said. But it is to say something significant, and significantly different – and wider – than we usually mean when we say that God loves sinners. It means recognizing that God is the one with a transcendent, unlimited 'talent for the makeshift'. God is found, in Christian experience, not standing on ceremony, not waiting until we get our act together, but eliciting unexpected redemption from the teeth of tragedy. That is why, right at the heart of the Gospel stories, there is a great surprise: Jesus goes straight into the midst of the most ungodly messes, where communities are infested with disease, impurity, evil and injustice, and invests God's love and renewal there.

If only we saw the same redemption touching every disaster. Time and again we pray for God's readiness to deliver us from the violence and confusion we bring on ourselves to appear more clearly and more often. Sometimes we wonder whether God is waiting for us to follow Jesus and be the bearers of his love into just such messes. Occasionally we see someone doing just this, though it doesn't look quite the way we would expect.

The television war correspondent Rageh Omaar, who had seen so much of the barbarous violence of Iraq, chose to pick out the extraordinary work of Canon Andrew White as the subject of a fascinating documentary film, *The Vicar of Baghdad*.[3] The portrait Omaar offered of White, who lives for much of the year inside Baghdad's heavily fortified green zone where he works for reconciliation, was a friendly one, even admiring. It so easily could have been otherwise. White could be depicted as naive, foolhardy, or even vain, pitching in – as he evidently does with relish – to a political and religious morass of untold complexity and risk. The resources he was shown bringing with him went little beyond his own generous bulk and boundless hope, his readiness to embrace as friends those whom most in the West see as sponsors of terror, and an extraordinary delight in being there, right in the midst of the bloodshed. In a word, he did not look in the least like Jesus – not the Jesus we normally imagine – nor sound like him. But he was there for God, loving the mess in his own distinctive way. Perhaps more of us could do that, in our own distinctive ways, instead of urging God to go it alone. The pattern of reaching out first, before the mess is sorted and the red carpet put out, is fundamental to the faith and the personal experience of Christians. St Paul summed it up: 'While we still were sinners Christ died for us' (Romans 5.8). The question we are left with is whether that pattern is also fundamental to our own actions.

Is acceptance enough?

I have been emphasizing the way God loves us with all our imperfections. This is certainly no new idea. Can it perhaps be summed up in the words, 'God accepts us as we are'? That phrase has become a shorthand for the gospel among many Christians. And for good reason: the awareness of being accepted by God can be liberating, especially for people who grew up with their own sense of inadequacy sharpened by a fear of God's severity. This language has touched parts that the language of sin and forgiveness did not reach. It has encouraged an *ethic* of acceptance, too, that we need to hold on to tenaciously in a society where the word 'bogus' is unthinkingly coupled with the term 'asylum-seeker', and where Jewish graves are routinely desecrated.

The turn of the millennium has distanced us from the 1960s; the clothes, the hairstyles and the slogans of that era look quaint and archaic. The modern culture of 'acceptance' has its roots in that era, and it is easy enough to mock it now, in these more hard-knuckled times. And it did sometimes lend itself to mockery. Some will remember the fashion for a form of 'acceptance therapy'. Its origins lay across the Atlantic, and it focused on the words, 'I'm OK, you're OK.' The words formed the title of a popular book written by an American psychiatrist, Thomas Harris, with the subtitle, *A Practical Guide to Transactional Analysis*.[4] There were some helpful insights in this approach, with its emphasis on the individual's deliberate decision to interact with others as adult to adult. But the phrase certainly left a great deal unsaid. As an eight-year-old I knew that picking on my friend was not 'OK', and after the event I knew that my outburst of fury was not 'OK', either. These small wrongs were distant relatives of the enormous wrongs that had swept across the world just before I was born, in the murderous years that Auden wrote about. The certainty that some things are not right, but need to be *put* right, is something we rightly cling to if we are not to slip into excusing and permitting violence and abuse, in and around us.

A more recent book, *The Spirituality of Imperfection*, suggests that we substitute another phrase: 'I'm not OK, and you're not OK, but that's all right.'[5] But is it all right? In the book in question, this capacious acceptance of ourselves and one another is seen as part of the response to addiction (the background of the book is in the principles and work of Alcoholics Anonymous). So perhaps the statement is dubious in theory, but practically therapeutic and effective. Maybe there are times when this seemingly straightforward and magnanimous acceptance is the way to 'love our crooked neighbour with our crooked heart'. And maybe there has to be something of this acceptance in the way we love 'our crooked selves', too. The recognition of the way things are for me – with all the limitations and difficulties that implies – can be a moment of hope rather than of despair. For many of us it is a very necessary point of turning away from the pretence that there are no such limits or from the Promethean and doomed attempt to overcome them all.

The advice of the Desert Father to a novice was, 'Go, sit in your cell and give your body in pledge to the walls'; Rowan Williams' comment on the saying links this ancient monastic counsel to our condition: 'You have to "espouse" reality rather than unreality, the actual limits of where and who you are rather than the world of magic in which anything can happen if I want it to.'[6] At the very least, some measure of acceptance can set our feet on firmer ground than the clouds of our wishful imagination.

At a traumatic moment a few words of acceptance and encouragement – 'Never mind' – are as good a version of the gospel as we can manage. At such times a verbal hug is more than welcome, even life-saving, a physical one even more so. In a similar way, the pastoral response to crisis or to self-rejection, delusion, addiction or despair may have to linger long at the point of simple, repeated affirmation: 'That's all right', each of us is lovable, even loved, as we are. The affirmation tries to express something more than lame resignation. It surely intends to stand for honesty and compassion, and to express one person's willingness to be with another in her or his need as entirely as possible. It is the intensive care of charity. And in the context of faith it may powerfully imply that this personal, human commitment is a sign of the unlimited, unseen commitment of God. 'If God is *for* us, who is against us?' – as Paul asks in his letter to the Romans, knowing the answer.

But, in the end, none of us does, or can, say 'Never mind' to everything about ourselves or others. 'I'm not OK, you're not OK, but that's all right' still leaves important things unsaid. To be close to someone – personally or professionally – who is gripped by addiction or hatred, or anything powerfully malign, is to be perpetually pulled apart by the two impulses: one to affirm the absolute worth of this person, the other to cry, to scream inwardly, for their release. Human judgement is hardly capable of knowing which impulse to obey at any given time, but at least we know better than to banish either completely. Within the confines of therapy – an Alcoholics Anonymous group or a counselling session – there may be a valid and deliberate choice to banish or confine one of those impulses, to offer the interpersonal equivalent of a 'special diet' designed for help and healing. But within the closest relationships, as in the immediate family, that option carries with it a sense of defeat, of having to settle for less than the whole me living with the whole you.

How many times have I heard preachers refer to 'unconditional acceptance' as the one defining quality of Jesus? And the phrase comes naturally to mind when we think of the countless Gospel stories of Jesus breaking through barriers and reaching out to *unacceptable* people. More than that, it expresses for so many Christians the wonderful awareness that Jesus accepts *us* without condition. Jesus does not say – to the woman taken in the act of adultery in John's Gospel, or to us – 'I shall accept you, forgive you, when you fulfil the following conditions.' He simply said, 'I accept you', or, 'Neither do I condemn you.' This may well have been part of what made him puzzling and offensive to upright Jews of his time like the Pharisees, people who believed in forgiveness but only after the sinner had abandoned sin. But Jesus had a great deal more to say. To the woman he went on to say, 'From now on do not sin again' (John 8.11). To the disciples who had betrayed him, the first words of the risen Jesus were, 'Peace be with you.' But he went on immediately to say, 'As the Father has sent me, so I send you' (John 20.21).

In other words, acceptance is a basic part of the gospel, but never the whole. Peter, the disciple, is depicted as one of the closest companions of Jesus. But, according to Matthew's Gospel, no sooner has Jesus promised him that he is to be the rock on which Jesus will build his Church than he rounds on him and says, 'Get behind me, Satan!' This was not in contradiction to the love of Jesus or the generosity of his forgiveness. Rather, it showed that the love of Jesus was full of hope and ambition for those whom he loved. When that hope and ambition were bitterly disappointed he could not simply say, 'Never mind.' The gospel is always about the tenacity of God's love, as well as its generosity; God has further for us to go than is implied by 'unconditional acceptance' alone.

As for us, there is no single, simple response available to us to cover every aspect of the imperfections we see and feel in and around us. In the Spirit of Jesus we have to discern when and where it is time to offer acceptance and when to steel ourselves for resistance. And we see this not only in chronic and intense difficulties but in more trivial matters, too. Do you speak gently to the high-spirited teenagers who have carelessly commandeered the pavement, and forced the old person to step in the gutter, or do you 'give them what for'? The choice is not simply between love and anger, kindness and hostility. For love – including the love of ourselves – differs from infatuation in this: that it is compelled to hold in tension acceptance, justice and hope.

Our deepest loving relationships almost always include some form of argument (whether we call it that or not) because we know intuitively that we cannot easily 'let things go' as we do in casual relationships. The deepest relationships are premised on the belief that I, as I really am, can abide in a bond of love with you, as you really are. The success of such relationships is premised on the acknowledgement that neither of us is perfect, but that we both have undying hope in and for one another. The arguments, and their happy resolution, are the expression of those three basic conditions of fidelity.

Yet there are times, too, when we would so like to live in a world that did not require such complicated remedies and routes to fulfilment.

The gospel of Jesus and the 'grace of the absurd'

'Bloody, bloody, bloody!' It isn't only children whose frustration boils over in angry protest. All of us, except perhaps those who have taken refuge in utter cynicism, have reason to protest – even if we learn to suppress the expletives. It is not only the messes that I and my neighbour get into that bother me, it is the difficulty and fragility of the means available to us to clear them up. Just as our hospitals are plagued with 'iatrogenic illness' – disease acquired in the process of healing – so our pastoral and political means of repair seem to create almost as many problems as they cure. Part of the attraction of a simple formula of 'acceptance' lies in its very simplicity.

One of the most appealing notions of childhood was the idea that a parent could 'kiss it better', and many of our religious and secular prescriptions for healing are fed by the yearning to return to that magical simplicity. To say 'Let it all hang out' or 'That's just your feng-shui', or even 'Smile, Jesus loves you' or 'God accepts you as you are', and then simply call it a day can seem such an attractive option. But the reality of imperfection keeps fracturing all these one-line solutions. The gospel's response is more than one line, because the gospel is incorrigibly realistic. But it also has one great advantage over these simple remedies: it is far more interesting, as I hope we can go on to see.

On those very few occasions when we encounter something – or somebody – that will change our lives we may react by an immediate sense of recognition, a heartfelt 'Yes!' But there is another possible response: puzzlement, irritation, even downright anger. Now if I exercise my imagination and try to think of myself being *there*, within the narrative of the Gospels, which way would I respond to Jesus? There are reasons for me to suspect that it would be in the second way, with puzzlement, even anger. The reasons are to do with the way Jesus is in the Gospels, as well as with the way my life is.

There is more that is unsettling, even shocking about Jesus (as the New Testament record shows him) than we usually allow. He is clearly capable of infuriating people, perhaps people like me. But when someone unsettles or infuriates us it is always worth pausing to ask, 'Why?' – even if this advice is usually best not offered in the heat of the moment. In the case of Jesus it is particularly worth pausing to ask, 'Why?'

My puzzlement – my indignation, had I been there – is because Jesus seems to be provocatively *unfair*. This unfairness of Jesus comes out in a host of ways. He told stories that were clearly intended to rub the point in, like the parable of the labourers in the vineyard who were paid exactly the same wage for doing radically different amounts of work. Most piquantly, Jesus puts the kind of reaction I would feel into the story we know as the 'Prodigal Son'. The elder brother, witnessing the lavish, apparently uncritical welcome home that his father gives to the younger brother – this selfish wastrel who has devoured half the family inheritance – gives vent to his bitterness: 'For all these years I have been working like a slave for you, and I have never disobeyed your command, yet you have never given me even a young goat so that I might celebrate with my friends. But when this son of yours came back, who has devoured your property with prostitutes, you killed the fatted calf for him!' (Luke 15.29–30). Yes, there are angles from which the gospel does not seem fair.

Perhaps this 'grace of the absurd' can best be articulated by another parable. This is not a parable hallowed by tradition but one of my own: a means to help fix in the mind a clearer picture of how Jesus is portrayed for us in the Gospels. Jesus behaves like a *dealer*, someone who trades – say, for example – in china and pottery. But he is a dealer who prefers 'seconds': soiled and broken vessels. What does he do at the sales? He bids high for flawed pots. What does he do when he has acquired them? He spends his energies and skill repairing them, waxes lyrical about them and gives them pride of place in his collection. To anyone who knows about china and pottery there is something provocative about this. Has this dealer, who appears to have deep enough pockets to acquire the most perfect specimens, no concept of the intrinsic worth of an item? Does he not see how important it is to recognize the value that lies in something unimpaired, unbroken? Does he not prize the care and effort that has gone into keeping it intact? This way of dealing undermines the basis of the market; it contradicts natural justice.

The metaphor of the dealer sums up several characteristic features of the stories of Jesus. To compare him to a 'dealer' is to suggest that he operated within a certain familiar 'market': in other words, he was not only a religious person, a devout Jew, but also one whose role or mission was recognizable as that of a religious leader, even a rabbi – however distinctive or 'unorthodox'. Yet the way Jesus spoke and acted in this context was not just unorthodox with regard to his qualifications or style (that he was not trained in a known rabbinic school, that he had a wandering, itinerant, ministry, for example), it struck deeper. There seemed to be a systematic difference between the way Jesus engaged with those who belonged to identifiable groups of observant, disciplined Jews (unbroken vessels), Pharisees and teachers of the law, and the way he dealt with people who in religious, cultural, physical and moral terms were obviously impaired. This was 'bucking the market' in every sense. In addition, Jesus clearly and consciously inhabited the whole world of Jewish belief, quoting its scriptures and observing its religious ceremonies, but appeared to challenge what was accepted as good practice within that world. In order to feel the force of who Jesus was, and is, we *must* somehow avoid sentimentalizing these basic aspects of his mission ('Jesus, friend of sinners'). To grasp its transformative power we have first to see how it offends and endangers our commonplace values.

In a nutshell, the way in which Jesus would have struck me as unfair is this. His total self-giving in identifying with the broken, in healing, forgiving, befriending and rejoicing with them, stands in sharp contrast to his harshness towards the more obviously upright and devout. Some Christian commentators think this is fun, pointing us to a gloriously topsy-turvy world in which 'respectable' people are made to look like fools and the 'ragtag and bobtail' are given the places of honour. And, it's true, this vision is no far cry from the Magnificat, in which Luke's Gospel sums up much of the meaning and promise of the good news ('He has brought down the powerful from their thrones, and lifted up the lowly' – Luke 1.52). But it had better not be the good news, *just like that*, or there is an end to all strenuous keeping of commandments, even the commandment to love, which Jesus told us to place above all others.

It is best if we keep puzzling at this aggravating matter, this grit in the oyster of the gospel. It may help us to avoid a number of 'one-line' ways of simplifying its message, which each miss the mark. Images of Jesus as the one who was 'a friend to all', or who 'showed acceptance to everyone', founder on the rocks of his fiery attacks on the 'scribes and Pharisees, hypocrites!' (Matthew 23.13ff.), and so does the old-fashioned picture of 'Jesus meek and mild'.

We may come closer to the truth, however, if we think of the unfairness of Jesus as showing that he was 'on the side of the underdog' or, in more theological language, he was exhibiting God's 'bias to the poor'. If we have to choose whether the gospel shows a 'bias' by God towards the rich or the poor, the comfortable or the oppressed, we must affirm that Jesus takes the side of the oppressed and underprivileged. The evidence is clear and often quite explicit – as when

Jesus told his disciples that for a rich person to enter God's kingdom was well nigh impossible (about as easy as a camel getting through the eye of a needle – Mark 10.25). But for readers like me, with more than one pair of shoes, and a comfortable house to live in, it may prove risky to treat this part of the truth as the whole. The risk is that this way of seeing the gospel may not challenge me deeply enough. If what the 'unfair dealing' of Jesus tells us is *only* that God prefers the disadvantaged then this may wake us up to the hideous inequity of our world, and even stimulate us to throw what weight we have into the attempt to set that right. But it may also lead us, mistakenly, to think of the poor or underprivileged as though they were simply the objects of God's favour. And it could lead us to think of ourselves as either right outside God's loving purposes or as only of value to God for what we can contribute to others. When Jesus met Zacchaeus (Luke 19.1–10) he was not only interested in the wealth he had to dispose of, he wanted more from the rich tax-collector.

I have been puzzling away at the unfairness of Jesus, because it seems to me to be central to the whole of his story and his work, his life and his death (there could be nothing more manifestly unfair than the crucifixion). This aspect of the gospel clearly says something about God's preference for the poor and suffering, it clearly says something about the way God mysteriously 'loves our mess'. But I want to uncover something here that is more creative and trans-formative than this; something that indicates how God's love might make a difference to our mess; something that is central to the way Christian faith is good news *specifically* in a world of imperfection.

The best way I can understand it is this. Jesus chose and favoured 'what is weak in the world' (as St Paul put it) precisely because there is a knowledge of what strength is that is given only to those who have known weakness, a knowledge of restoration and new life, given only to those who have known brokenness, a knowledge only the guilty have of freedom – of being forgiven and uplifted and cele-brated. Such is the knowledge that opens the way to fullness of life and to becoming the people we are meant to be.

The theologian James Alison writes about the process of 'un-hooking our hope from ourselves'.[7] This, he emphasizes, does not necessarily mean being brought to the point of despair about oneself – though that can surely happen on the path to renewal. Rather it has to do with letting go of our need to rate ourselves as 'good enough' to be worthy of hope. By impinging on the people he met in the unexpected, gratuitous and 'unfair' way he did – you might say, from such an acute angle – Jesus offered them a new freedom and hope that did not depend on how 'good' or 'bad' they felt or seemed in the world's eyes. Somehow or other we need the same 'unhooking' in order to enter into our full humanity. If and when our own imperfection ceases to be a matter of calculation and comparison ('Well, at least I'm not as bad as *him!*'), it can become a kind of opening through which we receive grace and hope from God. At that point, we are no longer comparing ourselves with others, and we begin to lose the need to get the better of others, or cringe before others. At that point we can begin to join in God's way of loving.

So then, the gospel way to real humanity is through a process and experience that includes two things: the recognition of our limitations and afflictions, and the blessing that changes them into sources of hope and compassion. This is the dynamic by which, in our personal lives, we sense God's Spirit making a new creation out of imperfect creatures. And this pattern gives shape to our identity as Christians just as clearly and powerfully as the Exodus – deliverance from slavery in Egypt and the crossing of the Red Sea – gives identity to Israel (see the book of Exodus, especially chapters 14 and 15). But this experience, this 'knowing', doesn't happen to us once only: it becomes the recurrent pattern of our lives and the source of our energy for good.

The Spirit, in Christian life, always comes most powerfully as a 'second wind' – like that surprising revival of breath and strength that comes to a runner at the point when the initial burst of energy is exhausted. Jesus gave that Spirit to the disciples ('breathed' it on them – John 20.22) after his death and resurrection and, equally importantly, after they had betrayed him and come back to him again. For them, there could be no mistaking *this* power to love as simply their own.

* * *

My wife and I had one young child and were expecting a second. Meanwhile, I was caught up in playing the role of a lively, energetic and self-sacrificial young priest – which I somehow managed to combine with finding time to spend in the company of (not unattractive) youth club members. I was drugged by the unaccustomed and heady experience of being useful to others, appreciated, even a little admired. I had acquired a new kind of power, much the better for looking so like goodness. In David Hare's play *Racing Demon* the vicar's perceptive daughter says of the young curate, 'He's thrown himself at the job. He's incredibly naive in that way. He wants to get hold of people and solve them.'[8] I, too, was a young curate.

Meanwhile, our marriage – which we, and our friends too, I believe, thought of as uncommonly romantic and happy – was suffering from my 'heroism' and from the pressure that people in the parish (wittingly or unwittingly) were putting on me. I went away for a short course to help my pastoral skills, although I didn't think I needed it. Near the end of the course, the tutor perceived that there was something wrong with and in me; how he saw it, I don't know. As I sat with a small group, the tutor drew out of me what I hardly knew myself, that I was outwardly 'doing splendidly', but inwardly riddled with confusion and guilt. In the end, he took a piece of paper and wrote my wife's name on it, put it on an empty chair opposite me and said: 'Would you like to say to her what I think you need to say?' And say it I did, inadequately, but truly. Then, late at night on the day of my return, I had to say it again, but to the real person. Oh, what a humiliating struggle, but as healing as good surgery. And through it the process of the two becoming one flesh began to be repaired, renewed and deepened, with power that came from somewhere beyond us both. Both times, when I spoke to the chair and when I spoke to my wife, it was the fact that forgiveness – combined with judgement, not separated from it – was already there, offered to me even as I spoke, that made it both possible and (in the end) liberating to confess. And so, in a tiny but to me immeasurably significant way, the 'grace of the Absurd' had triumphed, and our marriage was having breathed into it the 'second wind' of the Spirit.

'A happy family life', as W. H. Vanstone wrote in his classic book about faith and reality, *Love's Endeavour, Love's Expense*, 'is neither a static situation nor a smooth and direct progression: it is an angular process, the endless improvisation of love to correct that which it has itself created.'[9] And this zigzagging course, the way of the yacht against headwind, is characteristic, I suspect, of every pilgrim's progress, every story of life in faith.

One aspect of this pattern which may seem improbable, on first sight, is that judgement is bound up with healing and forgiveness.

We are used to thinking of judgement as 'over against' forgiveness and restoration. The judge is someone who decides whether you are guilty or not guilty. It will be a poor judge who simply decides to 'forgive' a guilty person, though a criminal may 'throw himself on the mercy' of the court, or even seek a 'royal pardon'. Yet there are, also, liberating moments of judgement. When things are bad, personally or politically, it can be surprisingly cathartic and energizing to hear someone say it out loud – to be told that things *are* as bad as you really fear that they are. The most memorable and telling public utterance of the twentieth century, surely, was in Churchill's speech of 1940: 'I have nothing to offer you but blood, toil, tears and sweat.' He, of course, had the knack of making misery sound, maybe even feel, heroic. But instinct also told him that hope can only grow if it is rooted in honesty.

To translate this into personal terms, a good friend or counsellor may offer what we might call 'non-judgemental judgement' (when we use the expression non-judgemental we most often really mean 'non-condemning'). Like the tutor on my pastoral training course this person will not let you 'get away with it'. The attention and time that they give you waits calmly for you to acknowledge the truth of the matter. If you won't or can't do so, you will probably go away complaining that the friend or counsellor let you down, in much the same way that some of Jesus' devout contemporaries found fault with him. But if that unblinking compassion finds a hint of responsive truthfulness, then recognition and renewal, judgement and forgiveness are born in the same moment.

It is for this that Christians go to confession – though, sadly, not very many of us do. Perhaps more would ask for this if the Church gave a fresh account of what confession is. Traditional forms of confession begin by the penitent saying to the priest, 'I confess that since my last confession I have sinned in the following ways . . .' – or words to that effect. What actually follows may be a list of misdemeanours, small or great, long or short. More often, I think, what happens, and what should happen, is more by way of a concise and honest account of where I am before God and my neighbour at this time, especially of where I am *troubled* to be. This is not primarily a guilt-inducing process (though guilt is a significant part of the kind of messes we are prone to). It includes things that are getting me down, as well as things that I have reason to feel bad about. But it can never be just an extended moan, or a means of getting things off my chest, because it is an account given to Christ, as well as the priest, and Christ looks on me with a compassionate gaze that enables me to take responsibility ('*I confess*') in *hope*, to look in the mirror and see that 'life remains a blessing'.

The reality of imperfection and brokenness is universal among human beings. It may be arrogance on my part, but I cannot believe that other people are all that different from me. This does not mean painting a picture of the human race as woebegone and feeble. The Christian journey is better characterized as a path of transformation 'from one degree of glory to another' (2 Corinthians 3.18) than one 'from gloom to glory' – though it usually includes a bit of gloom. We all have neighbours leading mature, adult, joyful and generous lives. We know people with astounding talents, abilities and characters, who make us proud to be human. But when we get to know our neighbours better – even the astonishing ones – we get a glimpse of other things, too. Limitation, inadequacy and pain are inherent parts of all our experience, whether we wear these things on our sleeves or keep them to ourselves. The Christian gospel does not, most emphatically, hold out to some people ('the chosen'), let alone to everyone, the offer of a life free from inadequacy or difficulty. To use the language of Edwin Muir's poem from the previous chapter, it does not promise us a return to Eden. We will look later at where, in the end, it does promise to lead us. But for now it is enough to know that the gospel offers, quite specifically, 'faith, hope, pity and love'. These are some of the characteristic fruits of God's love for us in Christ. When I say 'for us' I must mean 'for everybody', if the reality of imperfection is as universal as I claim. The only limit on its effect would be the limit of our readiness to own that imperfection and to accept the grace that comes to meet it.

* * *

On further reflection . . .

That has set me wondering, maybe you, too. Is there a danger in focusing on 'imperfection' as a subject? Isn't it a bit like looking at the cracks on the surface of an old master painting, rather than the painting itself? It could just be that in almost making a virtue out of imperfection we lose sight of some things that really matter. Should we not, after all, be aiming for relationships without breakdowns, rather than dwelling on the good that *can* come out of a mess? Perhaps it comes down to a question of whether we see ideals as oppressive or inspiring.

3

Unlimited company: the glimpse of a Holy Communion

As a young man, Auden 'thought he had done with Christianity for good'. He thought of Christian faith in the same category as the Icelandic sagas, or Grimm's fairy tales: it offered the poet a rich quarry of myth and fantasy, but no more than that. Then, rather out of the blue, there came an experience that made him think again. It was on a summer's evening. He sat on the lawn in a small circle of staff with whom he was teaching at the time – and, to put it in his own words,

> We were talking casually about everyday matters when, quite suddenly and unexpectedly, something happened. I felt myself invaded by a power which, though I consented to it, was irresistible and certainly not mine. For the first time in my life I knew exactly – because, thanks to this power, I was doing it – what it means to love one's neighbour as oneself.[1]

A poem he wrote at around this time seems to touch on the same experience:

> Fear gave his watch no look;
> The lion griefs loped from the shade
> And on our knees their muzzles laid,
> And Death put down his book.[2]

Was this a mere daydream? This power that Auden felt, to love one's neighbour as oneself, and the knowledge that he was held in the same love by his neighbour: are these real possibilities? Or are they possibilities that can be realized for more than a few moments of wishful thinking?

Auden's reflections on this moment of transcendence were typically precise and realistic. He was quite specific about what kind of love he felt: 'My personal feelings towards them were unchanged – they were still my colleagues, not intimate friends – but I felt their existence as themselves to be of infinite value and rejoiced in it.' He was precise, too, about how long this extraordinary experience lasted; it remained with him, less intensely, for a couple of days.

For someone as down to earth, even earthy, as Auden, this was a particularly haunting experience. In the language of faith that he would use later, this seems like an exceptionally direct experience of *grace*. The 'grace of God' is often experienced as that kind of peaceful invasion that I can freely welcome but I cannot control. There was, of course, nothing 'religious' about this ring of teachers, relaxing on the lawn; they were no kind of church. But the experience of that evening was, for Auden, like the hound's whiff of a distant quarry. It gave him a magnetic inner compulsion to seek a community in which each member is known to be of infinite value. Occasional moments of a kind of social bliss or transcendence continued to be important to Auden. He describes a musical evening at a friend's house in *New Year Letter* (near the beginning of Part Three) in just this way. Such experiences tugged and nagged him towards the Church.

The Church has to be true to that vision, not only because of the human longing for a community that fulfils our dreams and aspirations, but also because this is how the Church is defined in its own 'trust deed', the New Testament. The first Christian writers write about the Church as 'God's work of art', the 'temple of the Lord', 'a royal priesthood, a holy nation, God's own people'. The way Paul puts it in writing to the Christian community in Corinth is stark and little short of astonishing: 'You are the body of Christ' (1 Corinthians 12.27; see also Ephesians 2.10, 1 Corinthians 3.16; Ephesians 2.21; 1 Peter 2.9). This is the community for which, in John's Gospel, Jesus prays to the Father, 'that they may all be one. As you, Father, are in me and I am in you, may they also be in us, so that the world may believe that you have sent me' (John 17.21). The calling and meaning of the Church is to be a true *communion*, a company of human beings who are wonderfully given a foretaste of the unity-in-love that characterizes God's own being – to share, even now, 'communion with the Father and his Son, Jesus Christ'. Should not this be a company where sin no longer reigns?

This simple observation, that the Church is meant to be a 'holy communion', is the starting point for a great deal of contemporary thinking about the Church. In recent writings, theologians have tended to use two words from the Greek to express this broad concept of the Church as 'communion': *koinonia* (Greek for 'communion' or 'what is held in common') and ecclesiology (from the Greek *ekklesia*, 'church'). Why complicate matters with Greek words? Because they link our thoughts about the Church today with a rich treasury of meaning about the Church, and about God, written in the Greek of the New Testament. Perhaps for another reason, too: because our English word 'communion' can be identified a bit too quickly either with a misty mood (rather as we sometimes talk of 'communing with nature') or else identified simply with the service which, in many churches, goes by that name. The basic content of *koinonia* ecclesiology is both grand and simple. It envisages the Church as a way of being together on earth that reflects the divine 'being together' of the Trinity – God the Father, the Son and the Holy Spirit.

There have been many theological attempts to 'sum up' the nature of the Church. This summing up of the Church as *koinonia* has the beauty of making *relationships* paramount – relationships with God and each other. It makes clear that the Church is not primarily a building or an institution, but a way of living together – a way of living that is focused in the sacrament or service of Holy Communion, but that involves everything the Church does. One more thing in its favour is that it is not the property of any particular church – whereas previous ecclesiologies have often been distinctively 'Protestant', 'Catholic' or simply 'my own'!

This doctrinal language helps to focus attention on the reason for there being such a thing as the Church. It points to the special significance of this community among other human communities. The Church is here, it suggests, so that God, and the living love of God, can be encountered, known and spread abroad on earth. Here is how an important recent report puts it:

> By the indwelling grace of the Holy Spirit, the church is created to be an image of the life in communion of the Triune God: and she lives in this world in anticipation of the day when the whole creation will be renewed and God will be 'all in all' (1 Corinthians 15.28). In every aspect of its life the Church reflects the life of God.[3]

A picture may communicate the same theme more vividly than words. The picture is the traditional icon known as 'The Hospitality of Abraham'. It shows three figures seated at a table, interlinked by their gestures and eyes. The picture can be understood in three ways: as depicting the visit of three angels to Abraham, described in Genesis 18; as an image of God the Holy Trinity (Father, Son and Holy Spirit); and as an image of the Church, gathered at the communion table. The picture is engaging and attractive. It also seems to reflect very directly that haunting experience of 'secular communion' which so moved Auden.

Doctrine, however, not only has to be attractive, it has to be true. Teaching about the Church, in particular, can be 'checked out' by experience of actual churches. The image of *koinonia* may offer an excellent blueprint for what the Church is ultimately intended to be. But if the blueprint can never be seen to be realized in practice, its credibility and value are undermined.[4] So we cannot simply take this exalted view of the Church on trust, or accept it in blind faith. We have, somehow, to check the visionary doctrine against its earthly embodiment – to ask the critical question, how on earth can the Church be this *koinonia*?

The holiness and brokenness of the Church

At this point we need to call on our own direct experience and to ask some questions of it. If you go to church, or if you wonder about going, do you see yourself as having this quality? Do you see yourself *participating* in this communion? I don't mean the sacramental service, I mean the way of being related and united with others that echoes the loving life of God. Equally, does your local church look like such a community? And when you read about the churches in national or international news, do they seem like this? And if you see neither yourself, nor perhaps your local church, nor maybe the churches worldwide, as actually modelling this 'communion', does that mean that each or all of these happen to be bad examples?

Some people are led to move on from one congregation to another in a seemingly endless search for a 'real Christian community'. Perhaps they, too, have caught the scent of a community of love, but no actual church seems to have bottled it successfully. Others never even begin to go to church because they know 'for a fact' that 'they're all hypocrites, every one of them'. Others, again, continue with a lukewarm involvement in a church that has disappointed them once too often, yet which they cannot quite bring themselves to abandon. Churchgoers or non-churchgoers, we all know something – often something painful – about the failings of the Church.

If this vision of the Church as God's *koinonia* on earth is to be credible, or useful, if it is to give us the key to make sense of, and have faith in, the very imperfect churches we know from experience, we have to find honest ways of filling the gap, and linking what seems like a grand idea with the way things strike us on the ground.

'The Truth is Two-eyed', a famous theologian once wrote.[5] And what concerns us here is to have a 'two-eyed' view of the Church. It is easier, on the whole, to alternate between one eye and the other. That way we can accept an ideal, 'divine' picture of the Church one moment, and switch the next moment to seeing it as an ungodly mess. That habit, of looking one eye at a time, is becoming almost instinctive in our age of spin and scepticism. We have come to assume that there will be a wide gap between rhetoric – the way a product or political party or company is publicly represented – and reality. If we are not careful, it becomes habitual to accept that gap with a sceptical laugh. But doctrine can never be allowed to become spin, nor preachers to be spin-doctors. We have to be able to *have faith* in the Church. And since faith is never to be confused with fantasy, that means that we must pointedly refuse to close *either* eye when we look at it.

A two-eyed view need not be '20/20 vision', of course. There may be things about the Church that are not too clearly 'visible'. In trying to understand how the Church can be a Communion that is truly Holy, and can at the same time be grievously imperfect, we are certainly facing a *mystery*. And this is a mystery not only in Ruth Rendell terms – something complex but inherently solvable, if we have got all the clues – but in another sense. Because the Church is God's way of being present and active in the world, it must share something of the inexhaustible depth of God's own character. In the end we may be able to love the Church (for all that is wrong with it) more than we can understand it.

Still, this sense of the mystery of the Church is no excuse for avoiding the hard question: how *can* an organization be the place where we encounter the holiness, the unity and the love of God and yet be human? After all, what is it to be human but to err? And all our experience of human organizations tells us that the errors of individuals do not disappear when they congregate. The short, theological answer to the question is, 'By the power of the Holy Spirit.' But on its own that kind of answer is more like an appeal to magic than to theology.

We can begin to tackle the question by thinking not about the Church but about Jesus. If we want to understand how God can be human we are bound to begin with him. We speak of Jesus Christ as 'God incarnate', meaning, as St John's Gospel expresses it, that the Word of God became flesh, became human, in Jesus (John 1.14). Now, in becoming human, God 'took on history'. The only way for God to be with us, here, in Christ, was to be with us *through time* and to be with us *in our particularity and diversity*. When we read that Jesus slept in a boat crossing the Sea of Galilee, we don't think, 'Jesus shouldn't have done that, he was divine, the Son of God!' Naturally, Jesus had to take time to eat or to fast, to sleep and to wake, to travel, to talk and to heal. Similarly he took flesh as a particular person, masculine and of Jewish race. When he met Samaritans he had to communicate with them across the difference of culture and religion that divided them from Jews. The truth and love that Jesus brought to us may be – I believe, was – perfect and unified, but in order to come among us, sharing our time and space, it had to 'diversify'.

The whole truth cannot be expressed 'at any given time'. Having perfect understanding and compassion for others would not mean that the totality of that understanding and compassion could be communicated in one moment of encounter. A meeting with one person at one time might call – then and there – for a word of forgiveness or healing; with another person it might demand a word of judgement or challenge. These momentary messages could express only one significant part of Jesus' whole view of a person. Taken on their own, each message might leave the hearer more aggrieved or more complacent than they would have been if they had known all that Jesus saw in them. He could express the whole truth, the eternal truth, but only phrase by phrase, action by action. The light of his wisdom and love could hardly be experienced as pure light in our atmosphere. The story of the transfiguration, in which three of the disciples see Jesus irradiated with dazzling white light, points within the earthly story towards his divine perfection – a perfection that could be fully known only after the story was complete. Up to then, the light could be seen prismatically particularized, broken down, into the specific 'colours' that time and place allowed.

The Church has this in common with Jesus – the head of the Church: that it has to *take time*, and to *deal with diversity*. And if we think of the Church as communion, *koinonia*, this communion will have to be realized over time and in diversity. If we can grasp this firmly and work out its implications, we may be one step on the way to looking at the Church with both eyes open. That should help us to avoid being vacuously pious about the Church, but also help to clarify the important distinction between what *has* to be messy about the Church, and what should not be.

Koinonia *and time*

The Church has to be a *historical* community, it has to exist in time. This may seem obvious, but its implications are worth thinking about. A 'historic' church is one like St John the Evangelist, Escomb. Set in a small ex-industrial village in County Durham, this little building, with its continuous life of prayer, goes back to the seventh century. But the most recently established Christian fellowship, meeting in a warehouse, is *historical* because human beings take time and make history in the process. We take our time to grow up, to fall in love, to learn and forget things and to be broken and repaired. The Church may hold and preach a heavenly and timeless message, but it has no other means to hold and preach this message than in a community where time is given to us to live and to 'en-flesh' that message.

Interestingly, this is not primarily about us being given 'time to learn' how to be better, or how to be Christian. Church life rightly includes teaching and learning, and it does, sometimes, work like a 'school for discipleship'. But when you belong to it you soon realize what a strange school it is. You are given your graduation certificate right at the beginning, the moment you are baptized. Because at that moment you are given authoritative assurance that you are 'an inheritor of the kingdom of God': from this moment there is, in a real sense, no further to go. Look at the other end of the journey, too, and you will see that those who have been 'practising' church members for many decades still find themselves repeatedly back at square one. In fact those whom the Church calls 'saints' have a (admittedly, slightly tedious) tendency to stress how little progress they have made on the path of love – and they mean it.

No, the Church uses time in its own distinctive way. It uses time to repeat. To be a mother or father is to repeat things time and again: 'Let's just take a look at you before you go out', 'Welcome home, dear, do you need a drink?', 'Did you really mean to say that?', 'Don't worry, we'll be rooting for you', 'Love you, sleep tight, God bless'. The parents' repertoire of repeats is governed by their role of care and concern and the beauty and fragility of the child's life. The Church's repertoire is governed by the gospel, and shaped by the tradition through which the life, the worship and the teaching of the Church has grown from the gospel.

Verbal repeats can soon come to sound mechanical. Worse, they can seem like nags, and the more pertinent they are the more annoying they become ('Don't forget to turn the lights off!'). When church life becomes wordy it, too, can become mechanistic or moralistic. In any case, the final thing that Jesus told his followers to repeat was not just a formula in words, but action accompanied and illuminated by words. 'Do this', he said at the Last Supper, 'in remembrance of me' (1 Corinthians 11.24, 25). So the Eucharist, the service of Communion, is rightly the *staple*, the central item, of the Church's repertoire. Here, in a series of actions with words or words enacted, the Church prepares for and repeats the symbolic meal in which Jesus disclosed the heart and meaning of his love. This rite sums up everything the Church has to say, and because this is a rite – a prayerful shared action – it *incorporates* us. We become participants – not audience but players. We become 'partakers' in the act of Jesus as he loves himself 'to bits' for us, his friends, and hands over to us the substance of that love, to touch our imperfections with healing, judgement and hope, and to nourish in us the vitality and the power to become our true selves – in 'doing this', like him, losing ourselves in love.

'Only in rites', wrote Auden in his last published poem ('Archaeology'), 'can we renounce our oddities and be truly entired.' Not only the individual Christian, but the Church, too, is 'entired' – to use Auden's characteristically quirky expression – at the Eucharist: it comes as near as can be to being completely itself, in *koinonia* with God. In Henri de Lubac's words: 'The Church makes the Eucharist and the Eucharist makes the Church.'[6] That is one reason why the Eucharist is sometimes called a 'foretaste of the heavenly banquet'; it is an appetizer for the kingdom of God. It is an appetizer, however, at a particular time and in a particular place; it doesn't float above the flux of events. Naturally enough, people who come to worship 'wearied by the changes and chances of this fleeting world' (to quote a beautiful collect from the Book of Common Prayer) may yearn for the Church and its liturgy to be an enclave of fixity, a kind of secret garden within whose walls the patterns, colours and even the scents of childhood are kept intact. Auden was one of those who abhorred the introduction of 'new liturgies' and 'modern translations' of the Bible that ousted the traditional language of the Book of Common Prayer,[7] which he had known all his life. But to isolate our worship from social and cultural change conveys, to most people, irrelevance and eccentricity rather than timeless beauty.

In the sixteenth century, amid great upheavals, the Church of England adopted the Reformation principle that worship should be in language 'understanded of the people'. After that initial shock in Tudor times, it took a further 400 years for the fuller implications of the principle to unfold. For the implications are that, in *every* way, the Church should engage responsively with contemporary society. Church and society are to share one language and so to be in continual conversation, though not necessarily in agreement. Even when thinking solely about the Eucharist this means engaging with a succession of major questions: should divorced people receive communion, or be allowed to be ordained? Do those who preside (priests and bishops) have to be male, and either heterosexual or celibate?

The way I have come at these questions makes them appear as problems, matters that make it difficult for the Church to maintain its unity in love – its *koinonia* – and make it even more difficult for the divided branches of the Church to recover unity. But if being an 'entire' Church means being inclusive, the same issues are cast in another light. Our society, particularly over the last century, has come to what might be termed a wider understanding of social inclusion. We have become conscious of the ways in which some groups or individuals get 'left out', and we see how harmful that can be. So much so, in fact, that it often amazes us today that past 'Christian' societies could not only tolerate but even encourage slavery, or the silencing and subjugation of women, let alone quite explicit racism and homophobia. Our own values and behaviour as a society are not above critical examination on many fronts, but we cannot 'un-think' our commitment to inclusion. In fact as contemporary European

Christians, it makes us distinctly embarrassed to recognize that the Church had to be prompted by the wider society to attend to some things that, you would think, were evident from the age-old belief – rooted in the first chapter of Genesis – that we are all made in God's image. It is the world that has led the Church in the recognition of the equality of women, for example, rather than the other way round. So the Church, in its teaching and preaching, its life and its liturgy, is bound to engage with the agenda of inclusion.

St Paul, writing in the first century, could argue forcefully that women ought not to pray – at Christian gatherings, presumably – without a veil on their heads. He sought (a touch desperately) for meaty arguments to justify his assertion, but in truth his strongest argument lay in the fact that for them not to cover their heads when praying would have been an unnecessary source of scandal to the people of the time. (Paul's arguments about this in 1 Corinthians 11.2–16 are probably the least theologically convincing in any of the letters regarded as authentically written by him and so, at least, offer some comfort to lowlier preachers and writers.) Even when Christians are in perplexity or doubt as to the right way to interpret the scriptures or the traditions of the Church, we are still challenged by the values of the wider society and have to consider what message our own practices give to the world.

This means that decisions about the policy of a church towards, say, baptizing infants from families who do not attend regularly ought not to be settled on the basis of internal considerations alone – considerations such as the way that the leaders of the church understand the meaning and significance of baptism. There is another level of 'meaning' involved, too. What will the implementation of the church's chosen policy signify to 'the world' – to those who meet it from the outside? Sometimes, while a church acts sincerely in ways determined by faithful reflection on the gospel, it is communicating messages that do not seem at all like good news to others. There is, of course, no rule that says that the Church – like Jesus – cannot or should not communicate negative messages to the world. But at least it should avoid doing it by accident.

There is, then, no way of being a Church in time that does not mean facing change – whether we approach it openly, or by stealth. And since this is pretty sure to cause confusion and conflict among believers, these things are in some degree inseparable from the vital *momentum* of the Church.

Just suppose, for a moment, that I have to preach on Sunday, and that the readings from scripture for that day are readings I have preached upon 20 times (or more) in the past. And suppose that I go to look out an old sermon, having run out of time to prepare a new one – not, of course, out of laziness or because I stayed up too late watching a Saturday night film! When I reach for a text from ten years ago, what do I discover? First, perhaps, a little sense of disappointment: I'm sure this seemed better at the time! Second, probably, a shaft of insight into the mood and circumstances of ten years ago: this sermon has the smell of its era, not of today. And third, by good providence, something arising from the readings that made me think then, and makes me think again, now.

Through time, those who restate, and hear and re-enact the message of the gospel are themselves being changed. The ever-living word – the repeated message – is meeting with that wonderfully plastic and fecund creativity that marks human culture, its language, its art forms, its hairstyles, its worries. So each repeat is also a variation. In faithfulness to Jesus and the pattern of truth and grace we receive from him through the centuries of apostolic faith, the Church has to be a miraculous *composer*, a kind of huge, corporate Beethoven or Lloyd Webber, taking a primordial theme, the redemption song, and rescoring it to match the resources and the crises of each time and place. Preachers try to offer their own examples of how to do this, but the process is a much wider one than that, involving the response of every member of the Church to the gospel and the changing agenda of the world around and within us.

But if that is true for the whole body, the Church, it is true also for each of us in our own journey. As each of us, baptized once, is being repeatedly bathed in the gospel, being rehearsed in the art and practice of living as receivers and givers of grace, so our lives, our personal aspirations and difficulties, are changing day by day. We may be seeking to play the same tune every day of our Christian life ('Love the Lord your God, and your neighbour as yourself'), but we keep on being given different instruments to play. The intimate spheres of personal relationships, our own places of work and leisure, our own ailments and pleasures, keep throwing up new challenges and openings that compel us to rethink and re-act what it means to be a receiver and giver of grace. We keep on experiencing new breakages, each calling for its own distinctive repair – and requiring us to acquire the new skills that go with that – from the same source of divine love. And our intimate world is bound up with an economic, political and natural world – a whole, vast environment – that never puts exactly the same question to us from one day to the next.

Koinonia *and diversity*

I never thought that I would visit Montevideo, but when I did it was as the guest of a Uruguayan Methodist and enjoying the hospitality of a Roman Catholic training centre. The other members of the group came from Scotland, Australia, the United States and Jerusalem. Each belonged to a different Christian denomination and, just as significantly, to a different 'wing' of the Church – 'high' through to 'low', radical feminist through to traditional male. We were called together to complete a task for something called 'Faith and Order', an undertaking of the World Council of Churches that works for the unity of the churches. The task was to write a booklet, together, setting out what Christians could say with one voice about what it is to be *human* in the face of all the afflictions and challenges of the contemporary world.

On the table in front of us lay the reports of half a dozen previous meetings, dealing with issues that affect our human condition, from developments in technology and artificial intelligence to the impact of HIV/Aids. Two things we could all agree on: we were not equal to the task, and our views were at odds. It was, after all, a kind of microcosm of the calling of the Church as a whole: a bit of a madcap venture, an attempt at creation of the kind Auden pictures in 'In Sickness and in Health' – making 'A living corpus out of odds and ends'. As each person round the table put forward their prepared statements and proposals the sparks flew. Naturally, we prayed together. But the Spirit did not answer by giving us anything like that supernatural quality of love that came to Auden's circle of teachers. We rubbed along, but we did not gaze at each other with 'love in our eyes', as one sentimental chorus puts it. We *were* given three things, however: the will to persist, the ability to laugh and the readiness to compromise. So, by the skin of our teeth, or more accurately by the grace of the Spirit of God, the document was written and agreed at the end of a week. I don't know what the others took away with them, but I took away a tangible increment in my ability to trust – to trust the Church.

There is no need to go to Montevideo to discover diversity. Even a small family has room for several varieties of chalk and cheese; how much more so a local congregation, or a worldwide fellowship? And the Church is meant to have an insatiable appetite for diversity – that is part of the meaning of the word 'catholic'. The ultimate Church is 'a great multitude that no one could count, from every nation, from all tribes and peoples and languages' (Revelation 7.9), and wherever the Church divides itself up, into denominations, or monochrome congregations, or 'network churches' of look-alikes or of the like-minded, it is distancing itself from God's intention – to unite all things in Christ (Ephesians 1.9–10).

Desmond Tutu famously characterizes the Church as the 'rainbow people of God'. This telling image sums up all the vibrancy and beauty of a truly diverse communion. A Church without diversity is pale and thin, as well as far from the kingdom. But the wonder of the rainbow is that it combines the whole spectrum of colours in a way that seems entirely harmonic and unforced. In human terms, our diversity carries an innate resistance to harmonization, a kind of obstinacy that we rightly respect and even relish. Languages and cultures, ethnic and political groups demand independence as well as interdependence; sometimes they have to fight for their own survival. This is the background against which the Church is called to realize the harmony of *koinonia*. The Roman Catholic Church could once enshrine that harmony in the Latin Mass – the common worship of every tongue – just as the Anglican Communion could once see the Book of Common Prayer as its common bond and possession. But the whole Church now looks for a bolder *ensemble* than that, one in which tongues can remain distinct yet voice one adoration, cultures can retain autonomy yet belong to one communion. Desmond Tutu's own ministry stands testimony to the hazards, the cost and the miracle of painting such a rainbow.

The parish where I worked in the 1980s, an old coal-mining town, looked relatively monochrome. But it still seemed like a minor miracle of *koinonia* when, at the bitter height of the strike, miners, both striking and strike-breaking, with their families met and ate and danced together at the parish party.

Diversity and time both present the Church with the same dilemma. The things that make it supremely difficult to exhibit that perfect *koinonia*, which comes from God and which is summed up in the Eucharist, are the very things with which the Church is compelled to engage. It is not malice or wickedness that sets this tough agenda for the Church to tackle, it is the ambitious reach of God's mission to reconcile and unite all things in Christ. In a world of change and diversity, of contingency, limitation and interdependence, 'all things' can be united only by a reconciling power that works more patiently and profoundly than we tend to think, encompassing divergences and conflicts as a symphony incorporates discords.

There are ways of being a church that hide that reality more or less effectively. One is to be a 'denomination' or 'sect' where the unity and identity enjoyed by those who opt in is fenced about by custom or doctrine, by coded gestures or by explicit teaching, to minimize intrusive differences. The parochial system in the Church of England, which ought to stand for the inclusiveness of the Church (which is meant to be there for 'all the people of the parish') can be craftily distorted in this way – particularly in urban areas, where each parish church becomes a haven for one kind of Christian. Another way that this reality can be hidden is by maintaining a strong focus on authority and leadership over the church, such that tensions and conflicts can be 'kept under wraps' and be played out – to some extent – unofficially, while the public image of the church remains, theoretically at least, unquestioned. A third way is for church members to let all the challenging issues that change and diversity pose to a worldwide community pass them by, and settle for 'going to church' as private pragmatists.

But if two eyes are better than one, it is better for the Church not to try to hide what look like its problems. The 'problems' may, after all, be indicating the places where the Church is discovering new dimensions to its reconciling mission. Indeed, what we seem to have discovered in this chapter is that the call to embody *koinonia* in a world of imperfection is precisely what gets the Church into trouble. But if it is that call that gets the Church into trouble, the trouble is surely compounded by the ineptitude and even malice that we, members and leaders of the Church, contribute off our own bat. We have come back to the distinction between 'benign' and 'malign' imperfection – between, if you like, the limitations that belong to being human on the one side, and on the other the wickedness and confusion that bedevil our condition.

Human limitation, which is inseparable from the character, colour and richness of our story, means that *koinonia* has to be for the Church both gift and task. The Church cannot *be* a communion without perennially *making* communion. That is what God calls and equips us to do. Human wickedness and ineptitude mean that churches and individual Christians turn aside from that calling by strategies of avoidance, bigotry and sheer laziness. Sometimes we lack the will and the charity to persist in the hard work of remaking communion; sometimes we lack the wisdom and skill to do it effectively. So we find ourselves sacrificing the unity of the real Church for the sake of the church of our dreams. And the church of our dreams will always look preferable because it can enjoy *koinonia* without having to make it, which means that it will be able to sail on serenely without realizing – as the real Church does – its utterly desperate need for the reconciling, ground-breaking grace of God.

The communion of the Church is not broken by our differences. The Christians of the first century differed about what food they should eat, about whether or not they should be circumcised, about whether to observe special days of celebration or not, and much more besides. We differ about the role of women in the Church and about moral issues, like the status of same-sex relationships. None of these issues (neither the ancient, nor the modern) is trivial, and the differences are heartfelt and bitterly painful. In some instances it may gradually emerge that there is one right answer for all Christians, in other instances the same gospel truth may continue rightly to be expressed in different decisions or practices. Now, as then, the only way to handle such differences in the Church is by a combination of prayer, charity, honest debate (which means listening and arguing), readiness to learn from experience and some degree of compromise. The arguments cannot always be gentle, but then the Church's *koinonia* was never protected simply by civility or decorousness.

So there is much that we should refuse to be embarrassed about. There is right and proper labour and travail about the way the

Church lives out the *koinonia* of God with human integrity in human history. No, we should focus our embarrassment where it belongs: not on the trouble God gets us into, but on our narrowing of God's purpose and our refusal of the humility, generosity, perseverance and joy that God gives us to get on with it.

The tension and travail in its soul

Around the time that Auden was teaching in Herefordshire and felt, that summer evening, the reality of a kind of communion, Michael Ramsey, then a young theological teacher, was waking at night with his head full of thoughts about the Church. For lack of a better notebook, he noted his night thoughts on the walls of his bedroom – at least so tradition passed down by the cleaners had it in Lincoln Theological College, where he taught. Ramsey's thoughts were worth spoiling the wallpaper for. They amounted, by 1936, to a book that remains 'an abiding classic',[8] *The Gospel and the Catholic Church*.[9] It is a book fired by his passion for unity. And it offers a vision of the Church as a community shaped by the death and resurrection of Christ, not just an 'organization' but a *communion* animated by the self-giving of Jesus and renewed by the eucharistic gift of his body and blood.

The basis of that communion, for Ramsey, lay in the recognition that, in St Paul's words, 'one [that is, Christ] has died for all; therefore all have died' (2 Corinthians 5.14). What all Christians share, he argued, is that we have all died to our old selves, with Jesus, and received a new life in him. In that new life there was no room for claims to superiority, one individual over another or one church over another. Some of his contemporaries liked to represent their Anglican tradition as 'the best kind of Christianity', but Ramsey saw his church very differently:

> For while the Anglican church is vindicated by its place in history . . . its greater vindication lies in its pointing through its own history to something of which it is a fragment. Its credentials are its incompleteness, with the tension and travail in its soul. It is clumsy and untidy, it baffles neatness and logic. For it is sent not to commend itself as 'the best type of Christianity', but by its very brokenness to point to the universal church wherein all have died.[10]

'The universal church wherein all have died.' Ramsey saw that, in its own muddled and often painful way, Anglicanism could embody a truth about the whole Church and every Christian – that we find our identity and purpose under God in the very process of being broken and remade, of losing our life and being raised up in the company of Christ.

One more word is necessary. It might seem that belonging to this company of reconcilers, the Church, would be cheerless and burdensome. And so it might be, but it is not. The difference is praise. 'The Church with psalms must shout,' wrote George Herbert, 'No door can keep them out.' The Methodist Church is governed by Conference, a big annual meeting that can be as dour – and as argumentative – as any parliament, but following a long tradition at any time during the proceedings someone can stand and introduce a hymn that the whole assembly rises to sing, with gusto. To the new-comer it is unexpected and slightly surreal on first encounter, but the tradition conveys a powerful message and can, at times, be supremely moving. This, it says, this praise of God, is what it is all about. The gift of music, along with the gift of humour, these are among the most vital gifts the Spirit of God has given us in our grace-filled struggle to be the Church.

* * *

On further reflection . . .

Funny, isn't it, how Anglicans so often seem to end up justifying Anglicanism, while members of other Churches do just the same? In a roundabout sort of way, this chapter has ended up offering a kind of *apologia* for the untidiness and tension that seem to be endemic in the Church of England, and in the worldwide Communion of Anglican provinces. But what if I, the author, were looking from out-side this Communion? The tension and untidiness might look more like signs of a Church that has lost its way. Perhaps God requires every Church to reappraise itself in every generation as it seeks to be true, in its own way, to the gospel.

4

Dazzling darkness: God and silence, knowing and ignorance

The previous chapters have traced the theme of imperfection – how we respond to it and how God responds to it – in relation to our common human experience, in relation to the gospel and in relation to the community of Christian faith, the Church. But all along I have been writing as if God made all the difference. But what if 'god' were a word that carried no life, no power, no weight of real meaning? It is time to see whether, and in what way, that word can be given content: time to consider how we can know God – if indeed we can – and what it means to pray, particularly to pray in silence.

It was wartime and, in New York, Auden was beavering away at his task as a poet. For him that meant not just 'writing poems' but digging down into the deepest resources that his faith, culture and intelligence offered. He was driven by the need to answer the question that the war posed to him: 'If, as I am convinced, the Nazis are wrong and we are right, what is it that validates our values and invalidates theirs?'[1] He could still write 'light' poetry, but everything he wrote showed signs of this major quest. And in this quest the recovery of a Christian faith that could speak in his time of disenchantment was central.

Meanwhile another, older poet was watching over the rubble-strewn and smoking streets of London wearing the armband of an air-raid precaution volunteer. He, too, in the troubled years before the war had found his way to Christian faith. Like Auden, he believed that this faith was vital to the survival of culture and civilization through this darkest of dark ages. He, too, was a regular Anglican worshipper. His name was Thomas Stearns Eliot. For all these similarities, however, the two poets, linked in mutual respect, could

46

hardly have been more different in temperament. The difference came out in their religion as well as their poetry.

Typically, even on the darkest days Auden felt a call to rejoice. For him, love (human and divine) must always have room for forgiveness and shared laughter – the two belonged together. That is not to say that he took a simple, 'sunny' view of life. His faith and poetry equally tremble with doubt and with awareness of the sufferings of the world and of Christ, and yet hope and comedy keep invading even his most desolate moments. After years of preparation and work, he finished in 1954 a set of poems called *Horae Canonicae*. The title (which is Latin for the 'Canonical Hours'), refers to the seven daily acts of prayer and worship observed in monastic tradition, and the poems come as close to dealing with the day of the crucifixion, Good Friday, as Auden felt was possible in poetry. He shines an unsparing light on the human weakness and wickedness that lead to the judicial murder of Jesus. Yet the final poem in the sequence, 'Lauds' (the early morning monastic service), 'shows humanity waking not to guilt, but to worship':[2]

> Among the leaves the small birds sing;
> The crow of the cock commands awaking:

The cock-crow, so often associated with the guilt of Peter, the disciple who betrayed Jesus 'before the cock crowed', has become part of the dawn chorus, an alarm clock for new life.

Eliot's vision, on the other hand, is starker and darker. He is a poet of ice and fire, of rigours and extremities. There *is* hope, even in the heart of his most troubled and depth-charged poetry of faith, but it is not a hope that dare raise its voice, let alone laugh. To explore the whole landscape of faith with Eliot as companion would be to enter on a harsh and eerie terrain (a 'Waste Land', to use the title of his great work written between the two wars) in pursuit of a rare and elusive satisfaction: the journey would need tougher boots than mine. Nonetheless, it is Eliot who proves an intrepid guide when it comes to seeking God in prayer and stillness. While Auden can light the way to praise ('Let all your thinks be thanks,' he wrote), it is Eliot who is the right literary companion at this point in the journey. 'I said to my soul, be still,' he wrote in 'East Coker',[3] and that instruction provides the central theme of this chapter.

Do we really have to pray?

A good companion is not always an easy companion, and having the poetry and the example of T. S. Eliot at hand at this point in the journey does not make it easier going. The particular character of Eliot's Christian faith and conduct often looked odd to his contemporaries; in our generation it seems remote and even alien. There is a great deal about his approach to God and prayer that can appear harsh and self-negating. At the same time, it isn't difficult to imagine the sheer irritation Eliot would have felt had he encountered twenty-first-century 'spirituality'. To put the contrast in a nutshell: when spirituality figures in our Sunday papers, it is usually seen as an aid to personal well-being, part of the project of self-fulfilment. In contrast, for Eliot prayer was more like the crematorium of the self. The two approaches seem poles apart, but the tension between them is creative, perhaps even vital, if we are to see how the prayer of stillness and the way of unknowing can be the basis for 'knowing God' in our generation. One thing that Eliot understood was this: that each generation finds distinctive ways of domesticating real religion or of pushing it aside.

Eliot lived towards the end of an era in which religion was naturally associated with discomfort – at least with bodily discomfort. There are still relics in our culture of the idea that if it isn't painful, it probably isn't doing you any good. And simply to kneel in the uncompromising pews of a traditional church for a few minutes may be enough to show that this idea has a long religious history. However, attitudes to the body have changed dramatically in most reaches of our society. And with this change has come transformation in the ways prayer and spirituality are regarded. At times it can seem that contemporary attitudes have turned traditional attitudes on their head.

In times past it was taught that we need to discipline our bodies and curb our natural concern for their comfort, in order to develop and strengthen our spiritual life. Now, spirituality is more often portrayed as contributing to a healthy lifestyle and to personal well-being. Meditation is commended as an aid to relaxation in a pressured and frenetic world; it takes its place along with diet and physical exercise as a component of self-enhancement, a contributor to 'feeling good'.

It is easy for people like me, who belong to the great untanned and untoned, to react cynically to the 'soul and body' cults and pre-occupations around us. And we should watch our language. Is this old regime, which taught people the outward habit of bending the knee and the inward habits of self-denial any better than today's spirituality? It frequently went hand in hand with an attitude of shame or neglect towards our own bodies. Is it so damaging if, instead of that, we treat ourselves as if we're 'worth it' and if we equally exercise and cosset our bodies because they are worth it, too? That old regime was linked with an old Christian tradition (and it is very old) that treated the human body with suspicion, as something like a wild animal needing to be curbed and domesticated. Policies for prayer and for child-rearing were conditioned by that tradition. But whatever valid insight that regime contained, it looks infected now. We can trace lines on a map of disease that connect it not only to prayer and upbringing but to all sorts of repressive and oppressive evils, ways in which people (especially male people) saw virtue in 'taming' nature, 'colonizing' tribes and 'domesticating' half the human species.

Under the old regime, there was a tendency to veil the body – in public by garments and in private with a complex disposition of respect and desire. For most people in our society, that veil has been removed – at least most of the garments have. The removal has its dangers, but at best it signals a new joy in the glory of the body, a new tenderness in respect and care for it and a new affirmation of sexuality as the natural currency of embodied creatures. We seem to glimpse once more what God saw in the beginning of creation: 'and indeed, it was very good'. We can happily recognize our kinship with the rest of the animal creation. With this new joy and tenderness come spiritual qualities too, new or reclaimed from forgotten ages of faith. We can glorify God for the fabric of our environment in its living diversity. We can return to our own patterns of prayer with a fresh concern to respect our bodies, not just to control them. And we can look afresh at prayer with a new intent: that praying may be a channel for the Spirit to bring us to wholeness of spirit, mind and body.

Here, then, is a meeting point between long-treasured spiritual traditions and contemporary aspirations. Silence, stillness and meditation can be seen as components of health. People of different faiths and people of no faith can find common ground there as we struggle to live well in a noisy and frenetic world.

However, there is a big 'but'. Prayer, for anyone who prays 'in the name of Jesus Christ', refuses to be treated as simply a component of health, or a tool for self-fulfilment. This is not just because the 'old regime' keeps re-emerging like a cantankerous grandparent, to accuse us of self-indulgence and to warn us that the love of bodies is not a simple matter (which, in truth, it is not). It is because prayer cannot be mainly about *me*. In order for prayer to be any use to me, it has to be, first and foremost, *not* about me, my health, my well-being or my anything. Something in me needs to bend – whether or not my knees do – if I am to learn to pray.

Think, by comparison, of wildlife conservationists. They spend long hours in disciplined attention and observation of the osprey or the stag beetle, and the satisfaction they feel in this shines out. But the basic justification for what they do has to lie in the object of their attention, not in themselves, or their own benefit. The very heart of ecological concern lies in the inherent value of the environment itself, the natural world as a whole, and of the diversity of species within it. The fact that it is good for human beings to appreciate and spend time enjoying the world of nature goes without saying, but to put the benefit to *us* of environmental concern at the forefront is to stand the movement on its head and to reintroduce the source of the eco-logical problem (our human assumption that we matter most).

Prayer benefits human beings. More than that, there are moments when prayer becomes almost a basic means of survival, when things are so bleak that we have to cry out. But to think of prayer as an ingre-dient of a healthy diet or a rewarding lifestyle is to miss the main point, a point made starkly by Eliot:

> In order to possess what you do not possess
> You must go by the way of dispossession.[4]

Prayer is most fundamentally a 'way of dispossession'. It does not look like that to start with. It may at first look like a way of getting things, of enlisting God's help in grasping something we lack or something that is slipping away from us. It seems that Jesus encouraged this simple, almost childish approach: 'Ask, and it will be given to you,' he told his followers (Matthew 7.7). And surely some kind of asking-in-faith will always be a big part of prayer. But the practice of praying

has a momentum about it; it heads in a certain direction – away from
'me'. The very act of praying is magnetized towards 'dispossession',
to pray in the name of Christ is to be drawn steadily in that direction. I may start praying – in fact I often *must* start praying – with
my agenda, my own mental list of needs and priorities. But something happens when I place that agenda before God and then, even
fractionally, wait. This chapter is about that 'something'.

The necessity of silence

It was embarrassment that led me in the direction of this 'something'
that I have come to see as the basis of all praying: embarrassment
and a kind of mistrust. This was like the embarrassment of the
bridegroom kneeling for the nuptial blessing; he hears a gathering
tide of giggles from the congregation behind him, and the realization inexorably dawns that his mates have stuck a message of good-
will on the soles of his shoes. He had just been congratulating
himself on his cool demeanour and dignified appearance: he might
have known that he would somehow be shown up.

My embarrassment was caused by the inability to answer a simple question. I was working as a university chaplain, having been
ordained for four or five years, when I went with a group of students
for a weekend at a country retreat. While we were there, over the washing up one of the students asked me, 'How did you get to know God?'
If you are a chaplain, it is just the kind of question you should hope
to be asked. But it left me not so much with an answer as with a
shudder. Had I, in fact, ever 'got to know' God?

It was natural to assume that I had, in the course of theological
study, training and working as a priest, got to know God. But when
the question was asked directly, like that, I was not sure where to look
for an answer. It felt as if I had suddenly, belatedly, discovered a hole
in the middle of my ministry. In fact it was worse than that: the hole,
if there was one, was in my life as an 'ordinary' Christian. If you lack
the basic qualifications of a Christian, it is not easy to see how you
can call yourself, or be called, a 'minister'. Like the bridegroom, I had
always nursed an uneasy feeling that some time I would be 'shown
up', that I would be revealed to be a kind of spiritual fraud.

Looking back over the years, I think I can see the situation
more clearly than I did at the time. I don't think that I had, actually,

travelled all that distance on a false passport, as a 'pretend' Christian with no real experience of faith or of God. To say that would be to contradict the memory of so many significant moments in my earlier life. These were not 'thunderbolt' moments, but they had always seemed like genuine touches of God. What had happened, however, was that over time my experience of *human* relationships had grown and changed, almost beyond recognition. Having known, even as a teenager, all about infatuation, I had gone on to fall in love, to live in love and to start a family. In terms of personal growth, it had been the equivalent of moving from a bedsit into a house: I had discovered rooms of meaning, pleasure and pain previously unknown to me. And through all this, my knowledge of God had stood still. It no longer looked or felt like a relationship – now that I had found out so much more of what that word meant.

Very few are the times in life when we feel compelled to do something. Fewer still are the times when that sense of compulsion leads to *doing* something. My difficulty, at that crucial time when I was trying so hard to be a good chaplain, was that I could see the gap but had yet to discover how to fill it, or even whether it could be filled.

So much for the embarrassment – the shock of realizing that the emperor has (at best) very few clothes or that the chaplain does not *know* whom he is talking about. It is at this point that mistrust comes in. My own scepticism, my mistrust, would narrow down the options when it came to procuring some respectable clothes, or getting to know the God I talked about.

Some people eye every plate of food that is put before them with suspicion: 'I'm not sure that I'll be able to eat this.' Other people are naturally suspicious when they hear someone talk about knowing God, or Jesus 'personally': they are people such as me. Doubtless this mistrust has a good deal of prejudice in it; the kind of petty prejudice and waspishness with which people (especially clergy) in one wing of the Church defend themselves against the other wings. There was an element in this of shyness, and reserve too, a quality rather at home in the old days of the Church of England, where personal aspects of religion were kept from view. But there was a little more: there was mistrust, not of other people's but of my *own* religious feelings or 'experience'.

There were – indeed there still are – several reasons for mistrust of feelings, reasons that deserve attention here. How well do we know our own true and lasting feelings? I know that I can be carried away with enthusiasm for a cause, or for some music or art, or for a new-found friend, and that the passing of a mere week may leave hardly any residue of feeling or commitment. There are the passions of a sea cruise or a holiday or summer school: intense but insubstantial and anything but permanent. Lifelong faith, like lifelong marriage, needs to be built on something more durable than fleeting feeling.

That is one problem about 'religious feelings'; another is the question that is likely to haunt everyone who preaches or speaks (let alone writes) publicly about their faith. How *dare* I cherish or speak of my personal religious experience when there is still so much about me – in my mind and heart and actions – that contradicts the 'feeling' of God's touch? My heart may be touched, or even 'moved' by spiritual experience, but even as I treasure that experience I may contradict it by my behaviour. The words of Jesus, 'Not every-one who says to me, "Lord, Lord", will enter the kingdom of heaven, but only one who does the will of my Father in heaven' (Matthew 7.21), stay nagging in the back of the preacher's mind, as we feel the uncomfortable balance between on the one side our feelings and words about God, and on the other our Christian action and inaction.

Then there is a third reason for mistrust. How do we know that any feelings of ours are really feelings 'of God'? My feelings are, after all, close colleagues in the business of self-deception. It is my feel-ings that provide the evanescent, heady buoyancy that allows me to say, 'I'm fine, thanks', when I am actually attempting to fend off dejection or depression. Personal feelings do not only come raw and honest, but also 'cooked up'. And who better to cook up feelings about God than an ordained, paid, minister; not a charlatan, I mean, but someone who desperately wants to demonstrate more compellingly the reality of that of which he speaks and for which he is paid?

All these suspicious reactions might be swept away by one gust of real, divine wind. John Wesley famously felt just the compelling impact of the Spirit in a chapel in Aldersgate Street, and his heart was 'strangely warmed'. Perhaps Auden's experience on the school lawn in Herefordshire was equally self-authenticating. Certain experiences of God simply demand respect and response, point blank. But there remains, even then, one puzzling question that will not blow away. How far can any direct human experience tell us what God is truly like? Perhaps the only answer to that is, 'by being quite unlike any other kind of experience'. If the sun shines on my back I can feel its warmth and can probably guess its source, even if I can't see the sunshine; if someone I love returns from a long absence I can feel an emotional warmth and can understand its cause; but if I hear some words, not words about me or in praise of me but words about Jesus Christ, and my heart feels 'strangely warmed' the experience is 'strange' in two ways: first, because there is no evident cause for it, and second, because it is not like any other warmth I have ever felt. In fact one of the most frequent prefaces to any account of religious experience is the phrase, 'Words can't describe . . .' How could it be otherwise? Any encounter with God must share something of the total 'differentness' of God.

The only deity who could be credible to people who are aware of the light-year immensity of the universe and the immeasurable span of the 'history of time' must be *truly* God. That means the God whose 'space' is not vast but infinite, the God whose eternity includes all possible times, the God who 'dwells in unapproachable light' (1 Timothy 6.16). Such a God, in the words of the medieval writer Alan of Lille, may be likened to 'an intelligible sphere whose circumference is nowhere and whose centre is everywhere'. You cannot get your head around such a God, and any feelings we are given of such a God must surely be 'something else'.

The fact that God is known and encountered especially in the person of Jesus does not contradict this utter unlikeness to us, this *transcendence*, of God. When the qualities of Jesus in the Gospels are 'soft-focused' by our sentimental or wishful thinking, when we sing of him as 'meek and mild', or even when we preach about his 'unconditional acceptance', then we make of him someone more comfortable and manageable than his heavenly Father. But when we read the Gospels honestly we see the 'differentness' of Jesus. And Jesus' distinctive way of living, speaking, doing and dying represents very sharply the entire difference – the incommensurability – between God and our normal selves.

To revert to my own story: where then should I go in order to 'get to know' such a God? I could not rest satisfied with the immaturity and inexperience – for I had to recognize, that was what it was – at the heart of my faith and practice as a Christian. Neither could I build a personal story, a 'testimony' to God out of such experience as I had, at least not with any credibility. I might assemble the fragments, the luminous moments of providence, peace, judgement, deliverance that had come to me, into some kind of ramshackle museum of personal faith, like the drawer of old coins, beach-combings and cigarette cards I had squirrelled away as a child. But the moments of 'religious experience' I could recollect were, like the objects in that drawer, private treasures maybe, but with no public credibility, and no exchange value. They were also the treasures of a person who had changed, they were 'childish things'. I knew other people who had had knock-down experience of God, and even some who could speak of that experience in a way that showed that it was still living, not just a spiritual museum-piece. But I had to look for a fresh, slightly more grown-up, way of 'getting to know' God.

The upshot of this was that I discovered the path of stillness, the way of silence. That is how it had to be: everything I knew about my own imperfection and everything I believed about the inexpressible glory – the 'differentness' – of God pointed this way. I needed to seek silence not only in the realm of peace and quiet, the tranquillity that can come from 'getting away from it all', but a more fundamental and obscure silence of the mind, the heart and the spirit, too. I would need to turn off more than the radio. In order to 'possess what I did not possess', I had to be led 'by the way of dispossession'. In order to find a firmer foothold for the personal 'experience' of God I had to look, as it were, in the opposite direction: *away* from the realm of direct, warm, colourful experience, *away* from 'uplifting' feelings and 'inspiring' thoughts, and *towards* darkness.

I would, of course, be able to write about this way of dispossession much more convincingly if I had completed it, and 'got there', but as it is this can only be a report on a work in rather halting progress, a finding my way into the darkness of God.

The reason why we have to go this way is not because God was or is absent from this whole world of light, of positive and direct experience. The world of the senses is undeniably gorgeous; then and now it has always presented itself to me as, in the words of Gerard Manley Hopkins, 'charged with the grandeur of God'.[5] But the presence and action of God in the world does not come labelled. God's hand is normally hidden in the glove of contingency, of ordinary cause and effect. Faith looks to see God in all things and in every nook and corner of experience, yet seldom expects to pin down the action of God – and if it does, usually only after the event. In order to *know* your love for another person, you may need to be away from that person's physical presence, even from communication with that person by phone, letter or email: then, in what would seem to be the absence of the other, uncannily, 'heart speaks to heart'[6] and the substance of your love is confirmed. Can it be that in some similar way, to confirm our hesitant perception of God *in* the world, we need to look away?

This was not a path I dreamt up for myself. Countless others had trodden it before, although they tended not to be self-publicists, and their spirituality of silence never seems to be much noticed in the Church. It was not through their writings, however, that I was initially presented with this way of silence; it was through living witnesses. In one case it was two individuals, in the other, a cast of thousands.

A friend of mine had become a monk. As a person of refreshingly wide awareness and sharp wit, and not far different in age from the students I worked with, I thought he would communicate very effectively with them about prayer. It was agreed that he should come for a week with another young member of the Community, and the three of us planned a programme of sessions on 'learning to pray'. I saw myself, I remember, as on a par with the teachers, rather than the learners, in this programme. And it was true that I already knew some of the basics of prayer and of the use of silence. But as we sat in a circle in the coffee bar we had booked for our sessions, the carpet pockmarked with cigarette burns, I was being taken back to square one, to learn again what it really means to pray.

The other living witness came to me in France, in Taizé. The Burgundian countryside around the village is well wooded and hilly, great camping country, and that summer there was warm sunshine and an enlivening breeze. A dozen students and I had made it there by the Students' Union minibus and were enjoying the company of about 1,000 other young people from every part of Europe. But there was one aspect of the visit – my first time in Taizé – that marked me for life. Two or three times a day we would walk to the huge, dimly lit chapel, sit on the carpet and be *still* in the company of a huge con-gregation. The stillness started well before the words and music of the service; it carried on in and through the act of worship, and you had to drag yourself away from it afterwards, in time for the next meal. This corporate silence was like a placid, slow-flowing river on which our common worship was poised, and it gave to the worship, and to the whole experience of this vast encampment, a rare possibility of hearing God and each other.

These were strengthening, fortifying experiences. They needed to be, because the pursuit of this way of praying in silence needs fortitude. In fact it requires several qualities with which I am only rather modestly equipped, not least patience. And this way of dispossession is a long haul.

How prayer invites commitment

Most people in the street where I live do not bother about religion, or at least do not bother unduly about it. Even those who take the trouble to attend church quite regularly sometimes seem to detect a whiff of something unsettling when they hear phrases like 'getting to know God'. These reactions are usually put down (by clergy, at least) to people's half-heartedness, indifference or guilt. But just as there is a natural distrust of people who give ostentatiously generous presents, so there may be a natural suspicion of those who speak of 'costly commitment': is there not a hint of pretentiousness about the language? Part of my heart is with them. Part of my heart tells me that life is best 'muddled through' rather than lived with too much conscious deliberation.

The church I belong to – the Church of England – still caters for various forms of 'folk religion' (by this I mean the religious practices and attitudes of people who are 'not particularly religious' and who are not regular church attenders). If the 'C of E' caters for this wider population, it may provide a haven for those who see the Christian religion as part of their own particular way of muddling. And muddling is not in this case meant disparagingly. It stands for a pragmatic attitude to life that sidesteps big concepts and commitments. This kind of religion may be sparing in the use of faith language, but it may be perfectly big-hearted, and it is quite compatible with (and indeed often found alongside) heroic virtues in personal and family life. Given the choice, most people will not even join a political party, let alone a prayer group. This, however, has not in the past prevented them being involved, in some ways, with churches. At least, it has not stopped them being part of the Church of England, which has no constitutional way of drawing a clear line around its own 'membership'.

From the way our society has developed through the last few decades, it has begun to look as if this 'church for the uncommitted' was destined to disappear. According to most theological views of what the church should be, it *ought* to disappear. It makes for a clumsy kind of church, a community that somehow tries to combine the role of providing a national religion (for a nation whose soul is differentiated and sceptical, yet still partly Christian) with that of being a body of disciples, deliberate followers of Christ. Like any-one attempting to do two jobs at the same time, it can often seem to perform neither of them convincingly.

Yet for those of us who serve in this community, and who are mak-ing a stab at being active disciples, the combination is instructive. The church of active discipleship has a promise and challenge to hold up before the 'uncommitted'. It is, after all, possible (especially for English people) to be so bent on avoiding 'getting carried away' that they miss out on life itself. But the 'uncommitted' – those for whom the church is a component in a pragmatic ensemble for life, rather than the option by which they intend to shape their whole pattern of life – hold up their own warning and encouragement to the 'com-mitted'. They minister a peculiar but real kind of grace. This grace gently enquires of the eager disciple: 'Is there the faintest touch of self-importance about your commitment? We can see that it has led your brow to be furrowed and your chin to thrust, it has empowered you to say exciting things from the pulpit and even to stir up others, but has it helped you to love Uncle Joe? We had thought that loving Uncle Joe was meant to be part of this "discipleship" business.'

It is salutary, then, to bring the language of T. S. Eliot and the whole project I am outlining, of the 'way of dispossession', into conversa-tion with this questioning voice. To consider the pursuit – an ardu-ous pursuit – of a discipline of prayer charged with ambition to know God is to step decisively into the realm of commitment. And the ques-tion is rightly raised, 'Are you sure you want to go there?' This could be no better than chasing a wild spiritual goose, it could have a touch of self-dramatizing about it, and it isn't clear what advantage it has over muddling through. Prayer has its valid place in that muddling, after all. It can be a stand-by, always available to us in case of neces-sity, as a cry of pain, of desire and of joy: why look for more?

It has to be said that ours is an ideal society for people to mud-dle through. In wartime things look different, as they did for both

Auden across the Atlantic and Eliot in the blitz. In Auden's own words, written as he looked back on this time 30 years later, 'hair-raising things / that Hitler and Stalin were doing / forced me to think about God'.[7] The experience of war may lead some to lose faith and others to find it, but it must sharpen for everyone the questions that relate to faith and commitment. A critical view of our own society, by contrast, suggests that economic interests shape our common life in such a way as to arouse and satisfy our appetites for countless purchasable goods. The all-pervading business of consuming keeps us on the run, while it dulls our desire and saps our energy for wrestling with deeper concerns. Choices about meaning and about values become lost to view behind a welter of market choices. Put cynically, it suits those who make profits to keep us all 'muddling through'. Britons of European background (perhaps it is different for other faith communities in our midst) simply find it difficult, or nearly impossible, to regard questions of religious commitment as matters of life and death.

Yet for all this there are reasons to leave the path of muddling through and to enter on a steeper path of commitment; reasons not to let material comfort soothe away our hunger for heaven. There is, above all, the continuing murmur of the unquiet heart, which presses us on to seek God in prayer.

An unquiet heart

T. S. Eliot might not have liked to talk about his own 'unquiet heart' – he was a very fastidious man – but he would have recognized its reality. Just as Eliot's poetry can appear to a new reader as at once fascinating and impenetrable, so the personal mask that he cultivated was austere and mysterious. Lady Ottoline Morrell nicknamed him 'the undertaker' and another friend of many years, Virginia Woolf, referred to him as 'that strange man', who would come to lunch 'in his four-piece suit'. But behind the poetry and the mask there was a throbbing pulse of anguish and a fierce fire of imagination and experience. One identifiable source of anguish was his first marriage, to Vivienne Haigh. Entered upon almost casually, and very suddenly in the summer of 1915, the marriage soon took on the quality of a nightmare. They both depicted their relationship as a cage.[8] Ultimately, Vivienne's life became dominated by mental or emotional sickness. After years of separation from Eliot she was committed to a 'private asylum' where she died, unvisited by him, in 1947. For his part, Eliot, on 'escaping' from the marriage, had committed himself to a vow of chastity. Perhaps it is not surprising that belief in original sin held a key place in his religious understanding. Not that these personal sources of guilt and pain are what give authority to his poetry: the authority comes from the deep, universal resonances of his poems. Towards the end of his life Eliot enjoyed an Indian summer of contentment with his second wife, Valerie Esmé Fletcher, whom he married in 1957, and the sense of humour that had been very nearly invisible under the undertaker's cloak at last came to expression.

Here, then, is a life pregnant with affliction and struggle. The wartime view of South Kensington at night, its streets blocked by heaps of rubble, the smoke of the fire-bombs ascending and a great pall of ash descending, this provided a vivid symbol of inner torment, but also, for Eliot of the hope of redemption, restoration by 'that refining fire' which keeps flickering through the pages of 'Little Gidding', the last of the *Four Quartets*:

> We only live, only suspire
> Consumed by either fire or fire.[9]

There were two imperative requirements for Eliot. One was for purgation, cleansing. In an earlier draft of 'Little Gidding' he had written

> Fire without and fire within
> Purge the unidentified sin . . .

That purging, that burning away, could come only from God, from the God whose 'unfamiliar name' is 'love'.[10] But to draw near to that healing fire, something else was imperative: detachment, dispossession. It had become luminously clear to Eliot that the 'hair of the dog that bit him' was no cure for a lifetime hangover of grief and guilt. In other words, there was no route by way of his own feelings and emotions that could lead to the cleansing and healing he longed for. If he were ever to recover love in its human expression he would find it only through a path of detachment, a way that was apparently empty of feelings. That was the path he followed day by day as he knelt in St Stephen's, Rochester Row in the silence before the morning rush hour.

Eliot's life and writing is, in its peculiar way, high drama. Many lives, mine included, look tame in contrast. There are no bombers overhead and the fights going on inside, the inner traumas of guilt and confusion, are seldom so intense. But a modest life also encompasses cages that our own hands cannot unlock, griefs that time does not heal, and guilt that keeps blocking the way to a more truthful and generous love of others, and acceptance of ourselves.

I met quite frequently, through the course of a year, with a desperate, struggling (and un-cured) alcoholic. The intention was to help the alcoholic, but it was certainly instructive for me. Time and again I could feel in myself – like the 'pings' of a sonar device – echoes of the fierce submerged compulsions that demonized that person's life. It was made more and more clear that my 'ordinary' life hides an unquiet heart, a heart that can resonate only too sharply with that cry for immediate relief that the gin bottle represents to the alcoholic. Augustine has been proved right, time and again: our hearts are restless till they find their rest in God.[11]

It is an unquiet heart, ruffled, disturbed, frustrated by the impact of my own imperfection, which persistently presses me back towards the prayer of stillness, just as it was the disquiet of being found wanting that first compelled me. Seeking silence is an undramatic but powerful response to that restlessness, that disease of the heart. It combines realism and trust, because the person who takes this path is saying two things: 'Yes, this is where I am, a jumbled person in a jumbled world', but also, 'No, I do not have to flee this world or myself, nor resign myself to the jumble. If I stay just where I am, God can make all the world's difference.'

Just where I am

There is far more space within us than we imagine. Silence is able, gradually, to open up inner room. 'There should be in the soul halls of space,' wrote Jeremy Taylor, 'halls of space . . . where God walks.'[12] He wrote with the noisy conflicts of the seventeenth century ringing in his ears. In similar imagery Mother Julian of Norwich, three centuries earlier, was given a vision of 'the soul in the middle of my heart', which was 'as large as if it were an eternal world, and a blessed kingdom'.[13] Silent prayer, over time, has the capacity to unclutter our heart and mind and to give us interior 'room to breathe'. However, before it opens up this space for us, silence discloses just how badly we need it.

The first five minutes you spend in deliberate silence will most likely whisk you around on a frantic interior tour. This is a kind of shuttle trip, to and fro between the thoughts of a busy, anxious mind and a barrage of signals from your body. In the mind alone there prove to be several 'layers' of preoccupation. Beneath the obvious flow of consciousness ('What on earth am I doing here? What if someone were to see me here, sitting with my eyes shut?') there are bound to be 'don't forget' messages, with their ugly sisters, 'I *did* forget' messages. There may well be a tune playing somewhere down there, in a forgotten corner of the mind, or that vestige of a tune, a repetitive rhythm that finds itself auto-played in a muscular twitch or movement of feet or fingers. There may be some pictures, conjured from the memory or the imagination, and with each picture comes an unbidden and tempting invitation to watch the whole slide show. There is pretty likely to be a genuine train of thought somewhere, too, marked as 'what I am supposed to be thinking about', and probably leading nowhere. Meanwhile your senses have some surprises for you, as the body muscles in on the rare opening that being still has afforded. You might expect your body to object to being still and to keep registering protest itches and temperature readings. You might expect, too, that your ears and your nose would be delighted to keep you informed of traffic conditions on the road nearby, or the progress of the slow cooker. But let each part of your own body speak for itself for a brief moment, and a series of unexpected telegrams arrives. Eyelids send news of an involuntary repeating flicker and the eyes themselves of starbursts or colour-washes that somehow alight on the blank dark screen of closed lids; the jaw or neck informs you that it is held in a tense muscular lock that is wiring tension to the shoulder blades; the heart is pumping, even thumping away, seeking the attention it so seldom gets, and near the bottom of the tummy there are gripping pulses, never before noticed, syncopating irritably with the heartbeat.

We generally think that it is the busy world that prevents tranquillity, and so it may be, especially for city-dwellers and frequent travellers. But the attempt to be still shows my own body and mind to be a bedlam of activity. I am myself an overcrowded, claustrophobic site.

For stillness to happen, and a prayer of stillness, we need a practice that clears this inner claustrophobia, just as much as we need a place and time that is at least free from too much interruption or discomfort. As for the place and time, some people can find it only by going away from their home or workplace to somewhere apart, or by getting up at an hour when most people are in bed. Others are more fortunate and can earmark part of a bedroom or living room, and half an hour in the day, when they can be 'just where I am'. Rather comically, but effectively, in a house where we once lived I made the cupboard under the stairs my place to pray and to seek freedom from inner claustrophobia.

To find a place and time is one thing; to adopt the practices that lead to stillness is another. There is a certain artifice involved, a sense of training yourself. Simone Weil referred to prayer as 'the gymnastics of attention'.[14] For us, in our day, it may somehow be OK to put on the gear and go jogging, or visit the gym, yet still be embarrassing to engage with the physical and mental disciplines of prayer. But it is the common experience and witness of people who have prayed, across the generations and in other faith traditions, as well as Christians, that stillness in the presence of God does not just happen if you sit still and wish for it.

There seem to be three other simple practical requirements: a way of sitting (or kneeling) that is stable and stress free, a steady, rhythmic pattern of breathing, and some means to still the mind. The first of these can usually be worked out by trial and error; the two general rules are not to slump and not to cross your legs. Many people like to sit in an upright, supportive chair; I found that a small prayer stool (no more than a small wooden platform with two uprights to support it, which fits over the ankles and under the thighs when you kneel) suited me better. There is no special secret to the second – steady breathing – but it will probably mean breathing more slowly and deeply than usual. The third – a means of stilling the mind – is likely to be the most difficult to settle to and the least certain to work reliably. And before exploring the practicalities of this it would be best to make a convincing case as to why it is essential.

There are many ways of praying with an active mind. Most of the things we usually call 'prayer' involve some deliberate thought. It takes deliberate thought to thank and praise God, to ask help from God or to confess sin, although all these require more than just the mind – John Bunyan shrewdly observed, 'When thou prayest rather let thy heart be without words than thy words without heart',[15] which neatly puts the mind in its place. There is, however, a tradition of silent prayer, sometimes known as contemplative prayer, in which the mind, too, is intended to be still.

It may seem odd to try to suppress the activity of the mind. We are used to the idea that our minds direct everything we do, even if, at the same time, we often find ourselves doing the *last* thing we consciously intend. Yet there are good reasons to still the mind when we want to know God. One reason has to do with the 'differentness' of God. There are some very important things that we can think and say about God – that God is loving, just and generous, or that in Jesus we can see and understand all that can be seen and understood about God on earth. But having said these things and more, something else has to be added: the reality of God breaks open, spills over and utterly defeats all our concepts and words. All that we say and think about God can be no more than stubby fingers pointing towards the sun or arrows shot into the night sky: their direction may be true but they can never meet their object. To break off thought – the talking that goes on in our heads, as well as from our lips – can be to admit the reality of God. It is the gesture of a photographer who puts down the camera on being transfixed by the majesty of a mountain landscape. 'Here', we are saying, 'is that which I cannot capture.'

Our minds have a bossy tendency to imagine that they know more than they really do. This can be particularly damaging when it comes to thinking about God. In my head I can easily fix on one idea about God or one image of God and adopt this as 'my god' – or, indeed, believe that this is *the* God. Sometimes we form our idea or image from fear or from what we suppose to be reverence: then the dominant feeling about God is of judgement or dominance. Or the mind may entertain kindly ideas and images – of God as a protective father, a nursing mother or an intimate friend. We can find a biblical basis for all these thoughts and images of God, but taken in isolation, as if they told the whole story of God, they do not lead us towards God at all. My idea of God is always a cul-de-sac, a road that cannot lead me to encounter God's true reality. Ideas and thoughts about God are a bit like attempts to describe smells – an apt description may help you to recollect a smell, but no amount of description would enable you to experience a new one.

None of this is intended to deny the importance of *thinking* about God, or of words about God. The journey of faith would be impossible without the inspiration and guidance of the great biblical images of God: Abba, Rock, Shepherd, Shield. A few rare believers, like Thomas Traherne, enjoy in infancy a perfect sense of God's presence: 'My Knowledge was Divine,' he wrote. 'All time was Eternity and a Perpetual Sabbath. Is it not strange, that an infant should be Heir of the World, and see those mysteries which the Books of the Learned never unfold?'[16] Most of us, however, emerge from early childhood with few or no intimations of immortality: we only begin to believe and to pray with the help of the pictures or impressions those images formed in our minds. And Christians who want to grow in faith will keep plundering the Church's treasury of images and ideas of God, to explore them with imagination and with reason. This is a large part of what constitutes the invigorating business of 'faith seeking understanding.'[17]

Without doubt we need concepts and images of God, but we need to know how to use them and when to let them go. For me the key moment for letting go was when I needed not to talk to or think about God, nor to imagine God, but somehow to encounter – or better, to be encountered by – God.

So began a long journey that would lead me a little way towards a far country. But by what banal steps! The first step was to turn off the radio without provoking a panic attack. Under cover of 'liking music' I was habituated to having background noise as a sort of safety net around me. So I had to grow accustomed to the slightly spooky environment of a quiet room. Then I had to switch off my own auto-pilot, which always seemed to be set to either 'high velocity' or 'stupor'. This meant a moral adjustment, to accept that it is all right to be inactive while you are still awake (and not watching television). It also meant a new physical trick: staying absolutely still, deprived even of finger-drumming and foot-tapping. Then had to come the habit of rhythmic breathing – and a very gradual learning not to keep thinking about the fact that I was breathing. And then the stilling of the pulsating mind – which still, repeatedly, refuses to be still, after years of imperfect practice. Like other parts of the journey, this required trial and error, a process that led me to use the 'Jesus Prayer' – 'Jesus Christ, Son of God, have mercy on me, a sinner' – as a kind of mantra (a sound or phrase that is repeated over and over again, in time with breathing in and out, quieting the mind). Then I found that I needed an alarm clock – or something like it. Not because I was so deep in prayer that I was in danger of missing breakfast, lunch or tea, but because after ten minutes or so (maybe five, on a bad day) I would start furtively checking my watch to see whether my 20 or 30 minutes were up. A kitchen timer did that, but it had to have a silent tick!

The great spiritual books often miss out these banalities. Maybe that is because they are written by spiritual athletes who never had to bother with them; though more probably it is because they were written for readers who already had practical instruction or models of practice around them. But the very mundane details are important because they make clear what the deal is: that human beings – embodied, twitchy, self-absorbed, accident-prone – are given to know the presence of the eternal, all-sustaining God within them, beneath them and around them. And we are given to know this presence as human beings, not as creatures who are mysteriously beamed up into another realm, or become disembodied. In fact the whole idea (if I understand it rightly) is that we should em*body*, somehow or other, that transcendent and all-glorifying presence of God. Our twitches are not to be thought of as disrupting the Spirit's work in us, so much as signalling that it is in *me*, entire, embodied and imperfect, that God's love is being incarnated by stealth. Our accidents (which will not stop happening, however much we pray) are to become uncanny signs of providence, of the presence of the all-sustaining one. And if this is the deal, then our prayer, whatever depths it may open us to, will go on and on being a practical enterprise, including the struggle with toothache and tummy-rumbling, sleep and stiff joints, fantasies and (above all) pride at how well we reckon we are doing.

Having nothing and possessing all things

How should this chapter end, then? I would like it to end with a spiritual bang, not a whimper. But it can end only where the prayer of stillness seems to end. And although the wisdom of the ages suggests that contemplative prayer leads to the biggest bang of all, it is a very, very quiet one.

There are visions. But visions are not the end of this prayer. There are religious feelings – blazing exultation, copious tears, blissful rapture – but they are not the end, either. Things happen, of course, when we interrupt the surface traffic of personal life for any length of time. So silent prayer is bound to be an opening through which all kinds of experience can emerge. Grief can well up unpredictably into this space, or joy. We may sense some prompting, or a sudden and powerful insight may drop into the mind. Equally, while the mind is stilled, some awareness of radiance, or colour may seem to fill the space within us. Most of the time nothing remotely so 'interesting' will happen. But then it isn't meant to. The best advice about visions or religious experiences in silent prayer is something like, 'Say thank you, get down from the table and don't forget to wash your hands' – in other words, accept what you receive with gratitude, leave it to do its own work, and remember your own incompleteness.

The end of praying in stillness is 'to descend with the mind into the heart, and there to stand before the face of the Lord, ever-present, all-seeing, within you', in the words of Theophan the Recluse, the nineteenth-century Russian spiritual teacher who popularized the use of the Jesus Prayer. And the face of the Lord is not seen within us as light, or fire, or anything visible, but darkness.

> There is in God, some say,
> A deep but dazzling darkness –
> O for that night! Where I in him
> Might live invisible and dim.[18]

The shock at the heart of contemplative silent prayer is the shock of 'unknowing'. It is the discovery of an undreamt-of space and depth within us that we do not own or govern. In this space God is generously made known to us, but not known in the way we know things we can encompass; known, rather, in an illimitable, nourishing and transforming ignorance. The prayer of stillness aims for us to do no more than descend lovingly into this 'luminous darkness' and abide there.

This is not the whole of prayer. It is just one course in a balanced meal that includes praise and thanksgiving, confession and intercession; and it is a meal we take in company with the community of faith, not on our own. Neither is prayer the whole of Christian life. On its own, this prayer of contemplation could even become self-indulgent, like a private hobby. What if it gave me peace? That would be nothing if the peace did not overflow in patience and kindness when people's lives are fraying. What if it gave me faith sufficient to move mountains? That would, as readers of the New Testament know, be worthless without active, compassionate love. But set in the context of everything else that goes to make up Christian following – all the exploring, worshipping, working, grieving and laughing that go with stumbling along in the wake of Jesus – it provides a sure foundation, bedrock.

* * *

On further reflection . . .

Every time we talk about prayer, we come back to the same question. Who is it really for? So many ways of approaching prayer leave you wondering whether this isn't, after all, rather a selfish exercise. It may look God-centred, but it proves in reality to be rather me-centred. We have, of course, to take our own needs seriously when we pray. But I still hope that the way of prayer I have written about – the way of silence – is genuinely a way of making us, as human beings, better lovers and servants of God.

5

Salt of the earth: what kind of difference are we meant to make?

There is a memorial to Auden in Poets' Corner in Westminster Abbey. On it are carved two lines from a poem he had written as a young man in 1939. It was written in memory of another great poet, W. B. Yeats. The epitaph is taken from the closing lines of the poem:

> In the prison of his days
> Teach the free man how to praise.

These arresting lines express a great deal about Auden in a short space, and convey the spirit of defiance and hope that marked his heart and his poetry.

But is it enough? What does it signify to 'teach how to praise' someone who remains in prison? What about liberating him, and indeed her, from prison? The same question hangs over all that Auden did and wrote in his maturity. Quite early on, in fact around the time that he wrote this poem, he had come to a settled conclusion about his role as a poet, and about the nature of poetry. 'Poetry', he would often say, 'changes nothing': 'In so far as poetry, or any other of the arts, can be said to have an ulterior purpose, it is by telling the truth, to disenchant and disintoxicate.'[1]

Auden could be actively – even lavishly – generous in his personal life, but he distanced himself and his work, deliberately, from political and social involvement. It went further than that, in fact. Like Coleridge, he hated poetry that 'has a palpable design upon us'. He was obstinately suspicious of any attempt to influence other people's behaviour or the course of public events. As he put it in a poem of 1942:

Deliberate interference
With others for their own good
Is not allowed . . .[2]

It was as if there was a stark choice between two forms of writing: propaganda and truth-telling. Such was his preoccupation, maybe obsession, with truth and integrity that he would 'censor' his own poems fiercely, often revisiting them many years after their first publication, and – to the horror of his friends and critics – cutting out lines, verses or whole poems that he had come to feel did not ring true. Auden, you may say, required that poetry be the sworn enemy of spin, even if that meant abandoning, as a poet, any overt attempt to change society for the better. When it came to his reader, Auden said, 'I want his reaction to be: "That's true", or, better still, "That's true: now why didn't I think of it for myself?"' And his succinct definition of a saint was 'someone who does not lie'.[3]

There is something noble about such a rigorous commitment to integrity. It echoes the extraordinary sensitivity to moral precision that colours the novels of Jane Austen or Mrs Gaskell. The heroine (or just occasionally, as perhaps with Darcy, the hero) is often distinguished from others by this. She will not, or *cannot*, utter a word that might deceive or mislead, even when the prospect of future happiness depends on such a word. Or, alternatively, having once lapsed from truthfulness, she exercises ruthless self-criticism and follows a penitential and unswerving path of honesty, expecting no favours. Just think how strenuous this measure of integrity in personal morality must be, and we cannot help but admire it. In a nineteenth-century novel, it can invest the sheltered world of a Regency drawing room or a Victorian vicarage with dignity and drama, but how does it look in Auden's world, or ours? Unfamiliar and old-fashioned, certainly – but perhaps self-indulgent, too? At least, that thought struck Auden himself:

> The condition of mankind is, and always has been, so miserable and depraved that, if anyone were to say to the poet: 'for God's sake stop singing and do something useful like putting on the kettle or fetching bandages,' what just reason could he give for refusing?[4]

He goes on to explain that, in the midst of pain and crisis, no one *does* ask the poet to stop singing, quite the contrary. But (as he knew full well) the issue goes deeper than this and the question cannot be batted aside so swiftly. Poetry cannot evade judgement in the light of the challenge of human need and suffering; no more can religion.

In fact Auden's stance on the social purpose of his work is just a *bit* of a pose. Not that he is merely pretending to be concerned about truth-telling. He cared about it passionately. No, it is when he disowns any hope or expectation of changing the world through his writing that we can detect a hint of disingenuousness. We know, after all, that his orientation as a writer – the whole direction of his effort – was impelled by the barbaric tyranny and violence of the 1930s and 1940s. The development of his faith and his distinctive poetic voice was deeply conditioned by the experience of encounter with evil. There was a particular moment when it struck him with huge force. He was in a cinema in Yorkville, Manhattan, a largely German-speaking area of New York, in November 1939, soon after his move to the United States. A Nazi propaganda film was being shown, depicting the conquest of Poland. To Auden's horror, as Poles appeared on the screen, the cry broke out in the cinema, 'Kill them!' It marked the end for Auden of any easy belief in innate human goodness, and it confirmed a calling to go deeper, to dig deep enough to find a firm basis for understanding and resisting human malevolence. As he wrote in that same poem in memory of Yeats quoted on his memorial:

> Follow, poet, follow right
> To the bottom of the night . . .[5]

The words communicate a sense of urgency and of mission. It is a sense that breaks the surface repeatedly in Auden's poetry, particularly in the decade that followed. The mission is somehow to penetrate and understand the heart of the despair and darkness of the civilized human world and, having encountered those depths, to sing a song of hope there. This mission is profoundly spiritual, but also, ultimately, political, and it stands in tension with his frequent assertion that 'poetry changes nothing'. Rather, if this mission could be fully accomplished, the poet might influence nothing in particular, but would help to change everything.

Auden believed that (in Karl Kraus' words), 'Speech is the mother, not the handmaid, of thought.'[6] In the light of this belief, the poet's search for a language of truthfulness – which speaks of who and how human beings really are, and where our hope lies – this undertaking is not a cultural pastime, a kind of metrical Scrabble, but a fundamental contribution, maybe *the* fundamental contribution, to the building of a just and good society. Only people who can unmask deceit (their own, as well as that of others) without anger or retribution will be able to sustain a community of enduring peace. Auden's poetry, for all his disavowals, is intended to charm and educate us into being such people: people who have acquired a dialect by which we can speak, think and act truthfully.

So, after all, Auden's supposedly non-political poetry may be more 'relevant' than he pretends. It must be said, however, that contemporary critics did not necessarily see it that way. In the decades that followed the war, his work was increasingly to be accused of being 'cosy' and lacking social engagement. In the course of the 1960s, both politics and literature in the 'free world' were acquiring a new stridency, while Auden's poems were (overtly, at least) about subjects like hospitality and domestic architecture. Yet look closer, and time after time they still enshrine the same purpose and intent.[7] They mean to convey and instil a deeply moral politics, but to do it without any hint of moralizing. Stravinsky, who got to know Auden well when they were working together on the opera *The Rake's Progress*, for which Auden and Kallman wrote the libretto, said that he was 'the only moralist he could bear to listen to'. Truly, though he would never have admitted it himself, Auden possessed the art (and the compulsion) to evangelize without 'preaching'. This, he believed, was the only authentic kind of Christian evangelizing there is.

One more thing needs to be said about Auden's approach. As a young man at university in the 1930s he had shared, for a time, the political ideology that was dominant among intellectually adventurous people of his generation: Marxism. He had gone a long way towards becoming a committed socialist – though never actually joining the Communist Party, as some of his friends did. During the Spanish Civil War he went so far as to volunteer for service with the socialist forces, expecting to be used as an ambulance driver (though he recognized wryly that he would be more menace than help on a battlefield). The time in Spain was not a success. There seemed to be no useful role for him, and the chaos and barbarism he saw on his own side (the 'goodies') was quite enough to extinguish any tentative confidence he might have invested in political activism. He was not cut out to be a political or military belligerent. But this experience did more than confirm this; it contributed to Auden's growing conviction that ideology, and the action that went with it, was intrinsically toxic, contaminated at source by the failure to take account of original sin.

Auden's political journey was one that many others would make – often more slowly and painfully – after him. Sixty years after his Spanish experience of disillusion, the Colombian guerrilla leader Bernardo Gutiérrez found himself making the same discovery. Twenty years of armed struggle left him with the realization that 'there weren't goodies on this side or baddies on that side. We are all both good and evil'. So he determined that 'the revolutionary thing to do was to make peace'. And this was the object of his remaining years in politics, until his early death in 2008.[8]

Returning to Auden, how do we evaluate his journey of conviction? We have two options. If we take seriously the interpretation of his experience and of the bitter world around him that his poems and essays reveal, beneath their sometimes playful surface, his was the role of a prophet – a cigarette-smoking, city-dwelling and outwardly rather louche prophet, but a prophet all the same. So within this least radical-looking of writers we glimpse a heart of genuine radicalism. On this view he was a good deal more courageous than he pretended to be: he was seeking to understand and speak, and even in his personal conduct, to implement the truth, without which we perish. But there is the other option, too: say, instead, that what he was really doing was using poetic rhetoric and religious language to cover the tracks of a feeble retreat from active commitment? Taking refuge in a 'pacifism of convenience', had he persuaded himself that he was making a costly commitment to truth? Auden himself would not have tried very hard to refute the charge. After all, to do that would have required him to make an ideology of his own position. He would prefer to turn back the question with a witty line of self-deprecation. We are left to judge for ourselves, and critics of Auden have come down on either side in their assessments. But we are also spurred to ask the question for ourselves: how are *we* meant to make a difference in our social and political world?

Sometimes we might wish the question would go away; it certainly makes me uncomfortable. It has the overtones of a court summons, with the guilt that arouses even before reading the indictment. But it won't go away: 'making a difference' is a requirement, a proper criterion for judgement, for anyone who dares call himself or herself Christian. The tree, according to Jesus, is judged by the fruit it bears, and the one thing that counts, for St Paul, is 'faith active in love'.

Today, western Christians live out their faith in the light of a historical and critical awareness that has developed over more than two centuries. In that light it is impossible to forget that 'all that is needed for evil to triumph is that good men do nothing' (as Edmund Burke did *not* in fact say, but perhaps should have done!). So it is not credible to keep religion and politics in separate compartments or to view faith as a merely private matter. Had William Wilberforce, a great parliamentarian of the early nineteenth century, seen faith in this way he would never have led the movement to abolish the slave trade. It is not difficult to see that Christian faith and practice must make a difference to what we say to our neighbours and how we live with our neighbours, locally and globally. It is when we come to consider what *sort* of difference that we face some of the same questions that confronted Auden.

Many writers have considered the question as to whether there is, or should be, a distinctively Christian way of engaging in the political and social arena. Here, I am concerned with a more specific question. How does a Christian understanding of human imperfection – imperfection that marks everyone and yet always contains some seed of hope – affect that engagement? It was because of his sensitivity to this dimension, his deep awareness of original sin and redemption, that Auden's political and moral stance took the form it did. His 1940 poem 'In Sickness and in Health' showed how vividly he saw that the remedies human beings propose for our problems are infected by the same viruses as the problems themselves – 'how warped the mirrors where our worlds are made'. It was that insight that made political propaganda or even preaching so obnoxious to him. But what else does that insight offer, more than an excuse for sheer political scepticism and inertia? In the three sections that follow, I hope to show that it offers positive and creative benefits that our society badly needs.

None of us is infallible

'I beseech you,' said Oliver Cromwell to the Scottish Covenanters, 'by the bowels of Christ, consider that you may be mistaken.' The awareness that we are all fallible – and the readiness to admit it – is one of the fundamental touchstones of Christian political involvement. Not that you have to be a Christian to understand fallibility. In fact many people suppose that faith tends to encourage feelings of *infallibility*. When Tony Blair very cautiously admitted that his faith had a part to play in his decision to lead the United Kingdom to war with Iraq, he was immediately heard by many people as saying that God told him to go to war. Commentators were quick to see the spectre of religious fanaticism and to assume that praying about a political decision would inevitably make the person responsible more certain and inflexible about the decision. But what Blair actually said was that he understood his decision to be ultimately subject to God's judgement. That means acknowledging that the decision was itself no more nor less than a human one, a fallible one.

The perception of human fallibility is, for a Christian, bound up with the need to pray. If I pray over a decision, it will probably not be the decision whether or not to go to war. More likely, it will be whether to look for a new job or to stick with the present one, or whether to keep my mouth shut about some unacceptable behaviour I have just witnessed or to make an issue of it. I shall not expect to be 'told' what to do. Not because God never speaks directly to people – there are many unvarnished records of pretty direct prompting – but most of them (like my own initial sense of calling to ordination) come unbidden, not when looked for or prayed for. Much more likely, however, is that an intuition, an elusive but real sense of the rightness of one choice or the other will come to me as I pray, like a gift silently left on the doorstep. The choice that emerges will seem like 'what *I* have to, or ought to do', rather than a divine commission – it will not turn me overnight into a latter-day Joan of Arc.

Equally, praying about it may leave me with the awareness, all through the process, that it is *me* making the decision, with no answer emerging except that I might be right or wrong either way. That need not mean the prayer has been wasted, because after the prayer I will be left with an important awareness. That is a double sense: that I have been helped to take responsibility for my choices and – simultaneously – that the success or failure of what I have determined is entrusted to God. This outcome is not trivial: it is what helped Field Marshal Slim to sleep during the battle of Burma and – just as important – what helped him to avoid becoming a messianic egotist when the battle was won.

It is, of course, one thing to recognize one's own fallibility and another to own up to it. The story goes that Archbishop Geoffrey Fisher was held up by traffic and arrived late at the Vatican for his first, historic, meeting with the Pope – the first such meeting since the sixteenth-century Reformation. He apologized to his host, adding the words, 'But we're none of us infallible, are we?' Traditionally, the readiness to accept that we all make mistakes has been something of a British characteristic. But there has been a fascinating shift in our habits of self-presentation over recent years. Job applicants now inform us, 'I am a natural leader who inspires confidence in others and who can manage colleagues with skill and sensitivity.' Game show contestants confess, 'I'm a strong person who knows what I want and usually gets it!' The culture of public humility still emerges on certain occasions, when military or civilian heroes who have put themselves at risk for others are being interviewed, for example. But even among that archetypal body of apologizers, the clergy of the Church of England, the new language of self-assertion is heard. In fact it is required for success in the world of competitive appointments, where every parish seeks 'an energetic and visionary leader with a track record of achievement in building enthusiastic and successful congregational life'.

The shift in fashion has complex roots. One root is the recognition of the need for empowerment for groups who have been systematically disadvantaged. It is not difficult to see that the old-fashioned habit of polite self-deprecation, the trick of running oneself down in public, can be a good tactic for powerful people. If I am confident in my own strength, I can use the rhetoric of self-criticism or humility to disguise that strength and deflect possible criticism. Meanwhile, by teaching the same rhetoric to people whose position is truly weak, I can make sure that they stay that way. In other words, self-deprecation is all very well if life doesn't accustom you to take it all too seriously. One of the first moves in claiming a true equality among disadvantaged groups has been that they themselves affirm their God-given dignity. And it works. 'Who would have thought,' we find ourselves saying, 'that she or he would be out there, showing the rest of us how to handle such a tricky situation?'

However, the language of self-affirmation is available for use by those who have quite enough power already, added to which, they can afford the luxury of spin – which is the political technology of self-assertion. The handling of admissions of error, or still worse, weakness, in contemporary politics is highly sensitive, like the handling of radioactive material or salacious scandal. If there is too much of it around, it must be borne away by some self-sacrificial victim in a ritual act of resignation. It is hard to believe that a prime minister as recent as Stanley Baldwin, in the 1930s, could go on record as saying, 'I am a slow thinker, I need time to reach good decisions.' And would such openness about personal traits, weaknesses as well as strengths, be suicidal for a party leader today, or would it be a liberation?

There are two reasons why it might actually prove suicidal. One is because there has been such a widespread erosion of trust in our public life. The causes of this erosion were explored thoughtfully in Professor Onora O'Neill's 2002 Reith Lectures, *A Question of Trust*. One of the results is that people in leadership of any kind feel that their standing is fragile: to admit weakness, ignorance or error is to hand out ammunition to a host of eager snipers. So leaders seem to be driven to present themselves with a brazen confidence that hardly reflects their true self-image, while the media and public come to assume that all leaders are liars. This pattern of behaviour rooted in mistrust is not confined to national politics: it increasingly infects the culture of businesses, schools, hospitals and even voluntary bodies.

The other factor inhibiting honesty and candour in our public life is the yearning for certainty. It may be that as a society becomes more secular, so the level of anxiety for definite 'answers' within it becomes more intense. Certainly there is a shortage of the quality that Keats characterized as 'negative capability', when one is 'capable of being in uncertainties, Mysteries, doubts, without any irritable reaching after fact and reason'.[9] Where uncertainty emerges in our public life, it is assumed that the role of leaders, or experts, is to 'close it down', whereas if they were honest they would often acknowledge the uncertainty.

One of the repeated sayings of Jesus was, 'Watch, for you do not know . . .' The prayers, the comments and the involvement of Christians in public life should reflect that ability to be open and courageous about uncertainty. Faith in the gospel gives confidence in what is unshakable and, with it, the freedom to live with fallibility.

The perils of planning

In July 1942 Auden completed his 'Christmas Oratorio', *For the Time Being*. Fifty pages long, it combines poetry and prose, parts for chorus and parts for many soloists (Joseph, Gabriel, Mary, Simeon and others), witty songs and weighty verses. Originally Auden intended that the text should be set to music, and Benjamin Britten, with whom he was quite a close friend at the time, had promised to compose it. In the event, it was far too long and complex a piece of writing to be set to music. It would be many years before Auden acquired the self-restraint and skill needed to be a good libretto writer, as he proved in collaboration with Stravinsky (and with Chester Kallman), writing *The Rake's Progress*. It was not just indiscipline, however, that prevented Auden making a singable text in 1942. It was also that he had too much to say. For all its touches of music-hall frivolity, *For the Time Being* is energized by strong spiritual and political concerns.

Herod, before his massacre of the innocents (the event described in Matthew 2 in which all the children of less than three years of age in and around Bethlehem are slaughtered in the attempt to kill the Christ-child), is given a major speech in which these spiritual and political concerns are brought together. Herod depicts himself as a man of reason and enlightenment who has done all that he can for the common good.

> Allotment gardening has become popular. The highway to the coast goes straight up over the mountains and the truck-drivers no longer carry guns. Things are beginning to take shape. It is a long time since anyone stole the park benches or murdered the swans. There are children in this province who have never seen a louse, shopkeepers who have never handled a counterfeit coin, women of forty who have never hidden in a ditch except for fun. Yes, in twenty years I have managed to do a little.[10]

All Herod's good work, however, is threatened by the news brought to him by the wise men, the news of the birth of Jesus, of God incarnate. Herod contemplates what this will mean: the replacement of reason by revelation, and of justice, as the cardinal virtue, by pity, a turning upside-down of established orders, so that insignificant people feel important. 'Naturally', Herod concludes, 'this cannot be allowed to happen. Civilisation must be saved even if this means sending for the military, as I suppose it does.'[11]

Auden is consciously representing a perennial struggle. But it is not the struggle between oversimplified categories of darkness and light, good and evil. At the time when power and evil were as near as they have ever been to being summed up in a single person, Hitler, Auden chooses *not* to paint Herod, his political villain, as an evil monster. Instead, he portrays Herod as a 'liberal' who 'hardly ever accepts bribes'. He is really, we might say, 'quite a nice man'.

Auden's instinct, I suspect, is close to that of Gillian Rose, the philosopher. In her book *Mourning Becomes the Law*[12], she argues that we must not let ourselves think of the Holocaust in terms that separate it, and its perpetrators, from the way we view our own humanity. No: the moral and political struggles of history are always reflected – if only on a minute scale – in our own, and our misdoings differ in degree, not kind, from those inscribed on the most shameful pages of the past.

One perennial struggle is between control and letting go. Like Herod, we have our own objectives and goals. We make plans and dream dreams, and we often measure ourselves against the achievement of these goals. But then, if we are not very watchful, the success of our projects becomes a snare. In order to preserve the project (or 'civilisation', as Herod calls it) an element of brutality is brought into play.

Most of us can call to mind quite quickly the times when we ourselves have been hurt by that element of brutality. We have felt jostled, pushed aside or even knocked down by the juggernaut of someone else's ambition. Sometimes there comes a point, sitting around the table or sharing a drink with an acquaintance, when those painful memories begin to emerge in conversation, and that point marks the step from acquaintance towards friendship, friends being, after all, fellow sufferers, those who understand what we go through. We can all be sure when we have been hurt. But seeing and understanding when we do it to others is not so easy. Only in the most intimate and loving relationships does that kind of truth come out clearly – and in words that we can, just possibly, hear.

If we have ridden roughshod, cheerfully, over others, we are probably left as blithely self-confident as Toad of Toad Hall. But even Toad was eventually brought to book. In my own working life I can think of two 'successes' that were achieved with a cost to others that even I could not fail to notice. One was a matter of fundraising and building, the other of reorganizing. There was a tangible achievement in both cases. The new hall was built and the money eventually raised; the institution was given a new structure and shape. I could call to mind much less successful undertakings. But there was damage, too – the damage that is done by pressure and prolonged anxiety to all but the thickest-skinned of colleagues. It is that mixture of success and damage that makes these particular undertakings worth some critical reflection. This kind of reflection is hard to do: it stirs painful emotions. Nor can any one of us, look-ing back, comprehend all our own mistakes or inadequacies – let alone see where our failings end and other people's begin. What follows, therefore, is an honest, but only partial story.

Things happen to us when we aim to achieve something big. Anyone who has played the part of some small-time Herod – a leader with the best of all possible aims and intentions – will have experienced this. It is different with modest projects, or those I do not really care much about. But when the outcome matters, when I set out to tackle something of major importance, there has to be a personal dream. The dream is the product of a journey inwards, in thought and im-agination, as well as some doodles or cryptic notes on scraps of paper. It is by 'going within' that I can get the measure of what is at stake, generate the germ of a new goal, mull it over, refine it, envision it. That inward process may be sparked off by other people's ideas; it will certainly be fed and encouraged by them. But it has to be my own. I have to 'own' in my mind, heart and will what I shall com-mend to others and struggle to attain.

If I go on to commend this goal to others and they accept it, they will expect me to harness the means and the effort that are needed to reach the goal. So I put myself, or find myself, in the driving seat, with responsibility for steering the development and pressing the accelerator (the brake is seldom needed), urging and cajoling people to strive for the goal. Wise leaders may manage to delegate the role of driver without altogether losing oversight or ducking re-sponsibility, but it isn't always easy to see how, and it takes humility.

For the dreamer, firmly committed to the dream, humility can become a scarce commodity – and one easily mistaken for weakness.

Some dreams die soon after conception. A few gain momentum, and so they grow in potential for good and for harm. I can think of two 'dream' projects that seem to have much in common, but proved as different as triumph and farce: the Crystal Palace and the Millennium Dome. No doubt the project of building Paxton's ambitious glasshouse for the Great Exhibition of 1851 made heavy demands on the workforce, the planners and the financiers. From this vantage point (over 150 years on) it more than rewarded every ounce of effort. The Dome was quite another matter: it was built, that much can be said, but the cost was so great and the aim so trivial that few would dare call it a success.

Much of the harm with projects comes from the way the project – which is the visible expression of the dream – comes to seem like the one thing that matters above all. Goals are alluring. They raise the adrenalin and lift the spirits (some people's, at least), and they satisfy an almost primal urge to overcome inertia and chaos. But they take on a life and dynamic of their own, and this gives them the power to push 'obstacles' aside, even to make them 'disappear'. That is when injustices happen in the interest of the project, or people are put under extreme pressure. That is when the timetable for reaching the goal becomes itself an oppressive straitjacket. And this is when people are hurt.

When such things begin to happen, some mysterious and frightening forces may come into play. Almost anyone whose work has drawn them into the vortex of 'reorganization', in the health service, education, industry or local government, can vouch for this. Within the common life of the workplace or community where this is taking place, individuals are swept up by forces of aggression and fear. They find themselves, almost unintentionally, forming camps opposed one to another, or perhaps identifying 'blame' and seeking to eliminate victims. If you stop and try to identify and analyse the precise quantity of fault – the actual mistakes, misjudgements and unkindnesses that lie at the bottom of this unfolding process – they do not seem quite sufficient to account for the depth and painfulness of the mess. But no one can see a way to escape the maelstrom. In the midst of it one or two people, though troubled, are not 'caught up'. They grow in everyone's secret estimation. But most participants say and do more that they regret than at other times in their lives. Common humanity is reduced and personal freedom constrained by the power unleashed within the body corporate. If this happens (as I have experienced it) even among friends, how much worse it must be in aggressive workplaces or the unforgiving market place. The well-intentioned planner, with all his or her dreams and failings, has the power to unlock a Pandora's box of demons.

Jesus, in the Gospels, is tantalizing in so many ways, and he proposed and pursued tantalizing goals: foremost among them was the 'kingdom of God'. For believers this counts as the goal to end all goals, the Christian dream. But Jesus seems to avoid, quite obstinately, turning it into a project. The stories he tells about it show that it is worth *everything*, like the priceless pearl, that we should seek it before all else, and that it is bound up with God's justice or righteousness. But they also imply that its signs are seen in tiny things, like mustard seeds or the cure of one diseased limb, rather than in big schemes, and that what counts as 'fair' in this kingdom does not really correspond with our notions of equity. Above all, according to Jesus, we can fix no timetable for its achievement. 'No one knows the time of its coming,' he says, 'therefore watch!'

The fact that the Gospels give us such a suggestive and elusive range of ideas and images for the kingdom of God has allowed Christians to fill out the content of the phrase in terms of their own cherished ideals and projects. In the twentieth century the expression 'kingdom values' became almost synonymous with an egalitarian agenda for social justice. That agenda has its own validity, but it is not easy to see how the specific teaching in the New Testament about the kingdom validates it. Just as the story of the 'talents' (Matthew 25.14–30) was not told by Jesus in order to endorse market capitalism (whatever Margaret Thatcher might have told the General Assembly of the Church of Scotland), so the story of the workers in the vineyard (Matthew 20.1–16) gives no kind of blueprint for social democracy, as we envisage it today.

In fact the kingdom of God is a frame of reference that interrogates every dream and plan. We plan (in our better moments) to organize things so that people are justly rewarded for their efforts, while the kingdom sees those who have stood idle most of the day recompensed as if they had laboured all day, and the notorious criminal who repents as he is dying as its first entrant. We set targets for ourselves and rate our success against them, but the kingdom is always something being *given*, not achieved. We mark dates for implementation on our wallcharts, but the kingdom breaks in according to its own (God's own) inscrutable timetable – like the 'automatic earth' of Jesus' parable, which simply makes the stalks of corn shoot up whenever it likes. We are busy prioritizing our most important objectives, but the kingdom claims priority for the least, the smallest. In all these ways the kingdom is a giant, overarching corrective to our assumption that we can 'manage' or even that we know what are the proper aims of our managing.

However, if the kingdom is both tantalizingly and provocatively elusive, the person who proclaimed it is not quite so elusive. Jesus proclaimed the kingdom by his every action, not just his words – it is 'bodied out' in him, and in some ways can be seen in him. At the very least, by looking at the record of Jesus and paying attention to the way he behaves we can begin to get the hang of it. Just to take a simple example, not long before the end of his travelling ministry, the Gospels make it clear that Jesus determined that he must go to Jerusalem: he 'set his face' that way. This appears to have been as puzzling to the disciples as it was undeniable. While he is on the road to Jerusalem, a blind beggar calls out for help. People in Jesus' entourage try to shut the man up, maybe because they feel the urgency of this journey, but Jesus will not have it. He stops and summons the man, finds out his need and cures him. Then they both set off again – this time with the blind man also on the road to Jerusalem. (The story is told in Mark 10 from verse 46, and also in Matthew 20 and Luke 18.) It's a simple story, but an example of how Jesus shows that serving the kingdom is not shackled by ambitions and goals, however valid. The kingdom beckons in the interruptions along the road, not just at the end of the road. And disciples have to learn to stop, to put their plans on hold and to see the coming of the kingdom in the interruption as well as the goal.

Ultimately, the kingdom has to be manifested on Good Friday, as well as on Easter Day. It has to have failure – something more deadly than interruption – built into it. The form of success that Jesus preached and achieved can never be equated with the unqualified success of a human project or plan. The simple reason for this is that there are winners and losers in the achievement of our plans, and the respective satisfaction and pain that this involves is never entirely just. We may judge that the pain is justified by the achievement, but there will always be someone who knows otherwise, even if history obliterates that person's traces. The bigger the human dream and the greater the power to effect it, the greater the unmerited pain that seems to result – at least if the outcome of the great twentieth-century projects of Fascism and Soviet Communism are any indication. With the kingdom project, Good Friday makes it clear that the unmerited pain is born by God's anointed, Jesus himself. This is what makes the gospel such a strange and transforming prescription for the health of an unhealthy world.

The importance of failure

Charles Handy, broadcaster and writer on management, records among his most formative experiences an embarrassing failure in management. He tells the story in his autobiographical book, *Myself and Other More Important Matters*.[13] As a young Shell executive in Kuching in Malaysia, he came up with a brilliant proposal for petrol distribution to the far-flung settlements of this watery region. To replace the costly, inefficient process whereby small quantities were constantly being shipped up river in drums, he had storage tanks installed on the shoreline in each village. Now a single visit by a bulk-carrier steamer to top up the tanks would replace countless little delivery runs. But when, some months later, he set off on the bulk steamer to fill the tanks for the first time, the flaw in his plan became all too apparent. With the dry season, the water level in the river had sunk not just inches, but a hundred feet. The tanks were way above the reach of the boat's hoses and pumps. The tanks were retrieved and sold for scrap, the old delivery system reinstated.

Failure is shaming. Reading Charles Handy's story I can so readily imagine the feelings, impacting like body-blows, as the reality and magnitude of this massive blunder dawned. Where can I hide? What will they think of me now? Is that the sound of mocking laughter that I can hear all around me? How can I cover this whole thing up? These overwhelming sensations may fade with time. Recollected in tranquillity they may make the perpetrator himself chuckle: but not at the time.

This particular story is encouraging for several reasons. The first is that it is recorded by a 'successful' person. We need to know, and to keep being reminded, that the line between success and failure does not run between me and my neighbour – or my neighbour and me. Both experiences are our common lot, and the lot of prime ministers, refugees, saints and criminals too. Nor is it safe to assume that outward success is achieved by those who make the fewest mistakes. Being in the right or wrong place at the right or wrong time may have at least as much influence on our trajectories and on the way others view us. That most heart-searching of all Shakespeare's plays, *King Lear*, shows us an agonizing train of catastrophe through which the old king comes at last to see himself and others as they really are, and to understand the way of the world:

> A man may see how this world goes with no eyes. Look with thine ears: see how yond justice rails upon yond simple thief. Hark, in thine ear: change places; and handy-dandy, which is the justice, which is the thief? (Act IV, scene 6)

There is a good rule of counselling, which says that the counsellor should not invoke her or his personal experience to demonstrate that 'I know how you feel' – each person's situation and feelings are unique. But that rule may be slightly bent to good advantage when it comes to admitting failure. If you make your confession to a priest and receive absolution in God's name, it is then important to hear the last words the priest has to say: 'Go and sin no more, *and pray for me, a sinner.*' We are, after all, in the same boat, the priest is saying. In the same way it can be deeply assuring, when you are guilty and ashamed about messing up in some way, to know that the one you turn to for counsel knows about messing up from personal experience – even though you would probably rather not know the details.

Rowan Williams, in his book about the wisdom of the desert, *Silence and Honey Cakes*, tells the delightful story of a dialogue between Macarius, wise and experienced in the ways of God, and the less mature Theopemptus, struggling with the life of chastity and prayer in the desert.

> 'Do you not have to battle with your fantasies?' Macarius asks. 'No,' answers the younger man, 'up to now all is well.' Macarius's response to this is unexpected, to say the least: 'I have lived for many years as an ascetic and everyone sings my praises, but despite my old age I still have trouble with sexual fantasies.'[14]

The old man goes on to admit all the fantasies that assailed him until, at last, Theopemptus is able to own up too. By genuine humility and openness, the 'successful' teacher of prayer was able to release the novice from self-deception. The story can hardly be used as a model of contemporary counselling, or even of sacramental confession, but it shows beautifully the way that failure can become a vehicle of grace and truth in the Christian life.

There is another way in which Charles Handy's story is instructive, and it has also to do with owning up. On returning to base in Kuching, he realized that his credibility as a manager would need rescuing urgently. If rumour of his expensive misjudgement were to be passed up the hierarchy of Shell management, it could be disastrous for his career. His decision was to make a clean breast of the matter with his local staff and to ask them to help him avoid any further blunders. It seems that they never whispered a word to higher authority: 'Instead, they gave me a chance to redeem myself, something that doesn't happen too often in organizations, although it should. That was more loyalty and understanding than I deserved.'[15] This was not the only possible way for him (or them) to respond. It must have taken courage on the young man's part. But this courage was itself honoured in the loyalty of the people who worked with him.

These are some of the simple, but powerful, arts that imperfection teaches. To recognize that to err really *is* human, to look at other people with clarity and compassion in the light of that recognition, to be prepared to put our own cherished projects on hold, to learn how to confess without self-deception or self-dramatization, to enlist each other in the cooperative business of ameliorating our weaknesses and maximizing our power for good, these are techniques so elementary that it seems odd to write a book about them. Odd, too, that it should be a book about religion and faith. Except that we know, most of us through some painful experience, that our difficulty lies not so much in understanding all this as in living it out. As when attempting to assemble a flat-pack cupboard, we do not need written instructions so much as present help, guidance and encouragement.

Since this is a book about faith, it intends to be pointing, all the time, away from itself towards the real source of that help, guidance and encouragement, the source for which there is only one

meaningful – though inadequate – word: God. God, who was present in Jesus and is present in the Holy Spirit, makes way through
human fallibility, mismanagement and failure, and opens that way
to us.

By way of shorthand Christians often call this the 'way of the cross'.
The trouble with this phrase is that it is deeply evocative for some
but hollow and platitudinous for many. Worse than that, for people
who do not think of themselves as devout it has a kind of 'sacristy
smell' clinging to it. The crucifix itself – the archetypal symbol of
Christian faith – inevitably falls into the same category. How can it
figure in an ordinary, semi-secular yet not unchristian home? For,
unlike the images of the Buddha or Shiva, it is laden with too much
meaning to be simply decorative, while at the same time it is too
overt a membership badge of a society people's grandmothers belonged to. Like so much that is associated with the Church in a
society with a great Christian past, it is in danger of being jettisoned
neither on account of Dawkins and the advance of scientific material-
ism, nor because of the inroads of Islam or other faiths, but because
it gives rise to faint embarrassment.

Even those who cannot easily engage with the old phrase or the
ancient symbol can still grasp the truth and the story that enshrines
it. The truth is that the nearest we can get to seeing God, according
to the Christian gospel, is in a picture of abject human failure – the
scene of the legalized murder of Jesus. Looking closely at that scene
and at all that went before and followed it in Jesus' life, you may
come to see a mysterious kind of triumph and a profound, restora-
tive power at work within it. But one thing remains clear: *this* faith,
faith in the one who went through this catastrophe, is faith in the
unavoidable and potentially transforming reality of failure.

*   *   *

On further reflection . . .

Well, you don't have to be too bright to see what was going on in
this chapter! It fits in with the general condition of people who
write books: they tend to prefer words to actions. Naturally, since
they like words, they use lots of them to justify *not* doing very
much to change the world. In the case of this particular book, could

it be that dwelling on 'imperfection' allows all sorts of reasons to emerge for hesitating to do very much good? Or is it those who don't hesitate but who rush in without a second thought who are the real danger?

6

Imperfect evangelism: treasure in clay pots

———•◆•———

> If I were a clergyman what I'd find unbearable is to talk about
> what I believe. Press a button and a clergyman's bound to tell me.
> At once. Even if he doesn't know me very well. He has to tell me his
> innermost belief . . . That's what's undignified. That's why clergymen
> are funny, I'm afraid. Because they're not allowed to be private. They
> wear their inside on their outside.

So says Frances, in David Hare's sharp-witted study of the Church,
the play *Racing Demon*.[1] It was first performed in 1990 and some
things have changed since then. The word 'clergyman' sounds dated,
for one thing. For another, it isn't just the clergy who are 'not
allowed to be private' – not about faith, at least. Most lay Christians are unlikely to be called on to preach from the pulpit. But
nowadays all of us, ordained or not, are repeatedly urged to share
our inner faith more confidently with our neighbours in the conversations of daily life. Evangelism, in other words, is every Christian's business. But here, too, imperfection has its part to play. Not
all preaching – whether in the church or in the supermarket – is
preaching of the gospel.

The thought of being 'an evangelist' does not appeal to everyone
in church. Mention to a group of churchgoers the need to be bolder
in talking about personal faith or letting other people know of your
own commitment to Christ and you see heads drop immediately in
a gesture that says, 'I'm sure I ought, but do I really have to?' There
can be many reasons for this. It may be because the group members
are churchgoers more than believers, people attached to a habit
rather than holding an identifiable faith – a faith you might talk about.
But it need not be that. It could be sheer reticence, or the same feeling that Frances expressed in the play, that very English feeling that
talking openly about deep inner convictions is 'undignified', almost

rude. Each of these possible reasons is open to change, in principle at least. The churchgoer can 'find' belief – maybe discovering that it was lurking under the surface of habit all the time. The shy can grow in confidence and openness and even the English can shake off reserve, if this is demanded of us by the love of God and the need of neighbours – neighbours who, in a secular society are increasingly cut off from the possibility of any sane religious hope.

There is, however, one further possibility, another reason lying behind that embarrassed cringe that comes over so many Christians when called on to 'gossip the gospel'. It could be that, clearly or obscurely, they sense that evangelism is not quite so straightforward a business. Knowing, as most do, that they are imperfect Christians, it may be not only a personal unease they feel, but a spiritual or theological hunch that there is something not quite right about this kind of summons to personal evangelism. That is the kind of hunch that I want to tease out in this chapter.

Recognizing mixed motives

Martine was a visitor to Bedford, staying in the parish with her penfriend and family. She came to church with them and stayed for coffee afterwards. I had preached that morning and had burnt the midnight oil preparing the sermon. I preached, as far as I can remember, about the English love of net curtains and the way this contrasted with Paul's words (in 2 Corinthians 3) about seeing the glory of the Lord, in Christ, with *unveiled* faces. I suppose, looking back, the sermon was rather preoccupied with what was wrong with us and our faith. After the service, hungry as ever for approval, I was on the look-out for a bit of affirmation about how I had done. Affirmation from a graceful young visitor carried particular weight. She spoke simply, with a smile and in slightly halting English: 'It is very nice, I like it. But I am not sure: is it, how you say, the 'appy news?'

On reflection, it was not the 'happy news' – the gospel or 'joyeux nouvelles' – that I had preached that morning. I had worked hard enough at it, up late on Saturday night, again. But what had motivated my effort? I think I was more keen to write a good sermon than to preach good news. I was left with a sneaking suspicion that the criterion I had in mind for judging success was whether people thought I had preached well, not whether they had heard the good and happy news.

'And so what?' one might respond. 'As long as human beings are involved in communicating the gospel, there will always be mixed motives at work. Don't get an inflated view of your own importance: God's light has shone through glass more stained than yours!' And so, no doubt, it has. But a truth was borne in on me that Sunday – the truth that human evangelists find themselves persistently obscuring or distorting the word that they are called to proclaim. This truth has to be taken seriously. Apart from anything else, there are too many people around who want us to forget it. Parishioners, or congregation members – many of them, at least – want to think that their clergy are not stained. People in the pub imply the same when they apologize for swearing in the presence of a dog collar. Lay people, too, when they speak up for their faith or take on some public Christian ministry are (to coin a phrase) whitewashed with the same brush. Woe betide the preachers and ministers of the gospel if we come to believe, ourselves, in this wishful-thinking image others can impose on us.

It follows that those who believe that they were once sinners make dangerous evangelists. It is tempting for them to conceive of evangelism as speaking across a gulf – the great gulf that divides the unbelieving world from themselves. This gulf can provide the imperative for preaching the gospel (to rescue the lost, from the wrong side of the gulf) but it can also foster a mind-set that undermines the very character of the gospel. Thinking in terms of this gulf leads Christians to misrepresent themselves. Partly this is a matter of making out that my past, before I became a Christian, was comprehensively, mind-bogglingly wicked while my present is categorically different. But more importantly it is a matter of how Christian life works in the present.

There may be momentous turning points in a journey of faith, but Christian life can never be simply a state of 'having received grace/having been forgiven/having been born again'. It is, characteristically, a state of receiving grace, being forgiven, owning and exercising new life. This equates with the fact that imperfection, self-evidently, does not disappear after conversion, nor later on in the Christian life. It may be that, to the outward observer, a person's quality of behaviour has changed radically for the better on becoming a Christian or growing in faith. The person herself or himself can hardly fail to feel the exhilaration and liberation of such a change. At first the contrast may seem as night and day. But passing time brings re-evaluation. The person who has been 'born again' comes to see glimpses of God's light in the former life that had once seemed so dark, and to realize that God's grace still has a great deal more work to do, after that initial transformation. In time, the initial wonder of conversion appears as not so much a once-for-all infusion of new life, but rather the unblocking of an artery, through which life-giving grace can (and must) continue to flow ceaselessly.

William Wilberforce was 'born again', becoming a devout and serious Christian in his late twenties. He became a man who made Christianity look attractive. The word 'grace' sprang to mind when people described him. But while he exuded a charm, quickness of mind and delight in the world about him that most of his contemporaries found enchanting, his private reflections were rigorously self-critical. When he said to a beggar, 'I am only a poor sinner like yourself,'[2] he was not voicing a pious platitude but a conviction based on his daily self-examination. It was a conviction that made it difficult or impossible for him to shut his front door on anyone who came claiming his help: he had fellow-feeling with each. On a frequent, sometimes daily, basis he would note down a list of his faults and tot up the hours that, by his own exacting standards of Christian discipleship, had been misspent. Somehow, in this extraordinary man, a searching awareness of his own inadequacies in the face of God's love became a gateway to growth in holiness so that self-critical as he was, the sense of God's loving-kindness constantly renewed towards him came to suffuse his existence. Finally, near the end of his life, his son Henry could write of him: 'He speaks very little as if looking forward to future happiness; but he seems more like a person in the actual enjoyment of heaven within.'[3]

What does the person who is so suffused by God's continual forgiving and regenerating grace have to say as an evangelist? A great deal, no doubt, but none of it with the metaphorical full stop that punctuates some popular forms of evangelism, the punctuation that makes of personal faith a *fait accompli*, a finished article rather than an incomplete but living affair.

Something of that incomplete affair of faith, with all its halting humanity, comes out in the pages of Gillian Rose's extraordinary and compelling memoir, *Love's Work*.[4] On first sight, nothing could be farther from the world of Wilberforce and his evangelical friends. Her testament was written in the early 1990s, as Rose was undergoing treatment for the cancer that would soon afterwards prove terminal. One among many threads within this closely woven, compact book is about the understanding that 'to live, to love, is to be failed, to have failed, to be forgiven, for ever and ever'.[5] The spiritual tradition that teaches this is, she reflects, 'far kinder' than the fantasy-language she encounters in the literature of alternative healing. As she perceives it, this fantasy spirituality weighs us down with the promise that the individual can be healed only by embracing unconditional love. There is no place for the redemption of a 'normally unhappy life', such as her own.

Earlier in the book, Rose describes her first encounter with the indomitable Edna, a tiny, triumphant New Yorker who, aged 96, is still surviving cancer, with which she was first diagnosed at the age of 16: 'She has been able to go on getting it all more or less wrong, more or less all the time, all the nine and a half decades of the [twentieth] century plus three years of the century before.'[6] Edna, the cancer survivor, offers a distant reflection of Rose's own experience and aspiration. Edna believes in a kind of magic: 'the quiet and undramatic transmutation that can come out of plainness, ordinary hurt, mundane maladies and disappointments'.[7] And as Rose faces her own mortality, this magic is integral to her own understated but real faith.

The underlying 'problem' of grace

The key to a 'kinder' evangelism, which does not rub out imperfection but includes it, is *grace*, for grace is God's own kindness. But the experience of grace is not only the key to evangelism: it also creates the main problem for evangelism and for Christian attempts to bear witness to faith in words and actions. It is a good problem to have – the very best – but still a problem.

In common English, 'grace' goes with 'graceful'; both bring to mind the ballet dancers in *Swan Lake* or a delicately executed square cut on the cricket field. That world of meaning is not entirely divorced from the meaning of 'the grace of God', but it is a rather thinned down, aesthetic version of it. In the New Testament, especially in Paul's letters, grace is what characterizes the whole relationship between God and us fulfilled in Jesus Christ. The concept of grace acts as a fulcrum; it articulates the way God treats us and the way we are to receive and respond to God. A hydraulic lift operates by the power of water, God uplifts creation by the power of grace. This grace is God's distinctive way of giving, giving freely out of superabundant, generous love. It is an inherently forgiving way of giving, but it does not stop with forgiveness or with any generalized 'good nature' on God's part. It comes to particular people in the form of particular gifts for particular needs. So it is the means whereby Christians are enlisted in God's purposes for the world.

So far so good, but there is a subtlety about living in the grace of God that is easily missed, as there often is with other forms of 'giftedness'. If you compliment a child prodigy on her brilliant performance, you may get a surprisingly muted response, not because she is too vain to bother with praise, but because she feels that the credit belongs, in a way, elsewhere – wherever the gift came from. It is truly hers, yet not her own. In a similar way, Paul wrote of what he had done, then quickly added, 'Though it was not I, but the grace of God that is with me' (1 Corinthians 15.10).

This subtlety of grace does not constitute a general problem for Christian living. Even though it might lead you, gradually, to sense that every moment or event of life is a kind of God-given bonus, you don't have to keep harping on about it. Where it does become a problem is when we aim to communicate the gospel, to bear witness to our faith.

There is a fascinating, strenuous example of a Christian wrestling with this problem of grace in Paul's letters to the Corinthian church. If you read the two letters to the Corinthians in the New Testament you can tell that Paul is having a struggle, even if it is not very clear at first what the struggle is really about. On closer examination, it proves that there are several struggles going on. But behind them all, I see Paul as wrestling with this question, 'How can I preach with authority to others, and remain truly a Christian?' As C. K. Barrett puts it, in commenting on 2 Corinthians 4.5 ('For we do not proclaim ourselves'):

> Paul's position was a difficult one ... Paul could not deny his commission without surrendering the Gospel; nor could he practise his

vocation as an apostle without denying himself any personal status or privilege. His apostolic authority could be manifested only by the renunciation of all the commonly recognized marks of authority.[8]

As Paul understood it, the incredible, transforming event of being a Christian meant discovering new hope, company, freedom and love as *gifts*. These were gifts offered 'in spite of himself'; they were not to be in any way understood as naturally belonging to him or as 'his' gifts. Yet he found that these gifts energized his own deepest identity, galvanized his talents, and far from 'blowing' his mind, enlightened it. This he would try to describe as the work of the Spirit in him, or as Christ (the one who had died and risen) somehow living and active within him.

But there were two peculiarities about the new reality (he called it a 'new creation') that had overtaken him. One was that it could not be privatized. It was well nigh impossible to speak of it in the singular. There was a very particular reason for Paul to know this. When Christ had first 'knocked him over' – almost literally, on the road to Damascus – it was with the question, 'Why do you persecute me?' (Acts 9.4, see also 22.7; 26.14), and not, 'Why do you persecute my followers?' So the first information Paul knew about the risen Christ was that he was alive in other people – those disciples whom he had been pursuing. When he came to be baptized and to know the same life in himself, it would always remain a life shared with all the baptized, although it has to be said that in times of passionate indignation, as when he wrote to the wilful Galatian Christians, he could come quite close to forgetting this! It follows that the direction of every Christian life story, Paul's included, is from the singular towards the plural. It makes it difficult for any Christian to tick other Christians off, or to dissociate yourself from them when they are an embarrassment, as they not infrequently are. This, as Paul found with the recalcitrant Corinthians, made you tend to become more, not less, annoyed with them. But the same direction of Christian life, from singular to plural, also makes it difficult for a Christian to speak about 'my faith' as a singular, separate entity: there is no private ownership of Christ in faith, only and always a shared possession.

There was a second peculiarity about this grace of God that conditioned Paul's life and language: it was allergic to self-importance.

The primary way in which God had shown the redeeming power of grace to the world was the way of the cross, whereby Jesus (for believers the most 'important' person on earth) freely and purposely let himself be rubbished, treated as totally unimportant. Divine love showed itself to be divine precisely by this act of expenditure that Paul famously called 'self-emptying' (Philippians 2.7). Having been stamped with this character from its origins, grace would always be the same, the enemy of superiority, the friend of self-forgetting.

It is, of course, one of the ironies of the gospel that divine grace goes out of its way to find people to seize upon who seem to be naturally endowed with lashings of the wrong qualities. Part of the fascination of reading Paul's letters comes from the sense that, in this utterly brilliant man, the generous, Christ-like power of the new creation has to contend with someone massively prone to self-importance – and immensely touchy too. (For example, just see how the heat of molten indignation pours out of him in a torrent of rhetorical questions in 1 Corinthians 9; this was not a man with whom to have a relaxed debate.) How much more telling it is, then, when confronting the critics of Corinth who are merciless in belittling him and undermining his work, Paul sets aside the normal gambits of self-justification. 'If I must boast,' he writes, 'I will boast of the things that show my weakness' (2 Corinthians 11.30), because God had shown him, 'My power is made perfect in weakness' (2 Corinthians 12.9).

Much of the time, Christians of later generations have borrowed the gestures and words of Paul without wanting to grasp their heart and meaning. It is not too difficult to develop a verbal habit of self-deprecation to the point where it becomes Pavlovian: 'Oh, no, I couldn't possibly . . . !' The words trip out in response to any hint of praise or self-satisfaction; and they afford an inexpensive body armour for those – the majority of us – who find conflict and criticism unwelcome. But the logic of grace works at a far deeper level. This logic is at work in the image of 2 Corinthians 4, the image of the gospel as treasure being held in human pots of clay, or 'earthen vessels'. Paul here is not using the parsonical voice so effectively ridiculed by Alan Bennett: 'Under this cassock I am but a man like anybody else.'[9] He is actually talking about the necessity for those who bear and communicate the gospel to be 'distressed', knocked about a bit, if the gospel is to be seen for what it is, Light and Love from God. This particular message, he was implying, cannot be wholly refracted through shining human eyes and faces, or through the polished countenance of a successful sales representative. If the love of God was shown through the body twisted on the cross, the gospel can perhaps be fully conveyed only through people whose lives have been a bit battered and bruised, but who – and this is important – have been cured, not of all the wounds, necessarily, but of the desire to advertise them.

Aelred Stubbs, an Anglican monk in South Africa, lost an emotional and spiritual limb when he was forced to leave the country. Like other members of his community who had worked in South Africa (Trevor Huddleston among them), he had become personally entwined with the struggle of black Africans against apartheid. He became friends with Steve Biko, the first president of the South African Students' Organisation, and his family, a relationship he treasured more highly, I guess, than any other. The icon-like picture of Biko on Aelred's wall was a constant reminder of Biko's violent death in 1977, at the age of 30, when in police custody. Although Aelred had lived his adult life in the sheltered security of monastic life, he (as much as others who share that arduous life) had been battered and bruised. This, however, was not the first striking thing about him. What I found most striking was an air about him that I can only describe as delightfully conspiratorial. That air might be apparent when he would reach into the old cupboard in his cell and bring out a bottle of rather good whiskey – the gift of a generous visitor – with two glasses. But it was a more pervasive air than that. The way he listened, spoke and looked in company with another implied a being-together in some kind of shared, unfathomable joke. It was much more than a joke, however, it was delight in creation, and passion for truth and the felt reality of forgiveness, all attached to the name of Christ. Long years before (Aelred was in his sixties when I first knew him), he had let go of a good deal of comfort and privilege. I suppose the sense he gave was of someone like the man in the Gospels who has discovered the treasure buried in a field and has invested everything in buying the field – only it was shared ownership, shared with you, his companion.

Aelred was an evangelist, though mostly, I think, on a one-to-one basis. The reach of his friendship and interest in others was extraordinary in its geographical and social width. Here was a poet, there a political activist, here a woman priest, there a novelist, or cricketer, or psychiatrist, any one of whom might testify that they had found, or recovered, or just managed to hang on to Christian faith with the help of his friendship. Most of them would know his faults, as he knew them himself. But I believe they would share one other perception about Aelred too. I would call it his 'withness'. Back to that sense of conspiracy: the gospel spoke through him in a deep identification with those for whom he cared, an identification fostered by constant prayer for each.

The words of the gospel can be spoken by those who stand over against us. But the reality of the gospel is always the reality of God with us – Emmanuel – and it has to be incarnated in the form of identification with the hearer. There is room for prophetic judgement within that 'withness', that identification, but it is judgement from one who knows the sin that needs overcoming from *within* and who knows from within that God's grace is stronger.

It is true, as I discovered, reflecting on Martine's kind but honest comment, 'Is this happy news?' that human evangelists will find themselves persistently obscuring or distorting the word they are called to proclaim. We would; after all, we (lay or ordained) are only human. But the gospel speaks, not when the reality of our imperfection is disguised nor when it is paraded, but when we feel and know in that imperfection our bondedness with every neighbour and with Christ.

* * *

On further reflection . . .

You may well question my choice of biblical quotations here. Perhaps I have chosen too selectively. There is, after all, not much sign of this 'problem of grace' in the Acts of the Apostles. There the first Christian evangelists simply get on with it: telling people the good news that Jesus, once crucified and now risen, is Lord. It could be that the approach to evangelism in this last chapter is too concerned about the integrity of the evangelist, and not concerned enough that the good news is proclaimed. Do Christians really have to recognize their own weakness before they can be true evangelists?

7

The shadow of death and the light of grace

Our life, wrote Karl Barth, is 'like a tree marked for felling'.[1] The great, multi-volume Swiss theologian could be concise when he chose to be. When you see a big red cross painted roughly on a tree, you look on it differently from other trees. And you wonder how long it will be before the axe (more likely now, the chainsaw) is laid to its root. It may be that Adam and Eve, in the biblical story, would have lived for ever had they stayed in Eden. Outside Eden, one thing that is still more certain than taxes is death. It is, perhaps, the universal hallmark of human imperfection.

As he got older, Auden's body showed signs of wear and tear. No wonder: he had subjected it to 50 cigarettes a day, uncountable units of alcohol and a lifelong aversion to healthy exercise. His body was 'the Injured Party' as he put it in a poem written in his mid-sixties, 'Talking to Myself':

> Time, we both know, will decay You, and already
> I'm scared of our divorce: I've seen some horrid ones.

He wrote that 70 was the right age to die, but it came to him sooner than that, in 1973 when he was a mere 66. It came with a swiftness of which he would have approved, and not long after he had set down this haiku, which his partner Chester Kallman told friends was his last composition:

> He still loves life
> But O O O O how he wishes
> The good Lord would take him.

By nature buoyant and optimistic – at a deep level, if not always on the surface – Auden never ceased to love life. 'I have always felt', he wrote, reviewing a book about suicide, 'that to be walking this earth is a miracle I must do my best to deserve.'[2] His character and his faith both protected Auden from the disabling terror of death that haunts many people of vivid imagination. But living, perhaps even more than we do, in an age of anxiety, he himself was not free from anxiety. In a concise miniature poem, 'Progress?', he compares the Plant ('wholly content with the Adjacent') and the Beast (which can 'tell here from there') with us human beings:

> Talkative, anxious,
> Man can picture the Absent
> and Non-Existent.

Faith relies on the human propensity to 'picture the Absent'. Most fundamentally, it is only as we wake up to the fact that all things might *not be* that we can begin to sense what 'creation' means – the bringing of existent reality into being from nothing (*ex nihilo*, to use the traditional Latin expression). Imagination is the faculty that enables us to 'see' things as other than they appear to our bodily senses, and even to 'see' them as not existing at all. If this faculty can enable us to wonder how everything came to be, it can inevitably also make us wonder where everything goes. So imagination invites us to think about not being here ourselves – about death. For most people, the image of a blank in place of their own self is deeply unsettling. When Keats' mind dwelt on his 'fears that I may cease to be', he depicted the outcome in terms of cosmic aloneness and the negation of love as well as ambition:

> . . . then on the shore
> Of the wide world I stand alone, and think
> Till Love and Fame to nothingness do sink.[3]

Keats' words imply that, through imagination and fear, death casts a shadow back over life. It does more than threaten to terminate our journey, it puts in question the value and meaning of the journey itself. A person who is bereaved, especially after a deep attachment, often feels this sense of futility to an overwhelming degree. 'Emptiness, emptiness,' says the Speaker in the desolate early chapters of Ecclesiastes, 'all is empty. What does man gain from all his labour and his toil here under the sun? Generations come and generations go . . .' (Ecclesiastes 1.2ff., NEB).

There is no arguing with the reality of that experience – the feeling that death has evacuated life of weight and value. As the book of Ecclesiastes cannot be denied its place in the Bible, so the felt reality of meaninglessness cannot be, and ought not to be, deleted from the realm of Christian experience. It is not just a 'godless' experience. On the contrary, there are indications that it deserves a special place. The ultimate depths of futility are sounded by Jesus as he cries out to God in dereliction on the cross, 'Why have you forsaken me?', and some of the people we might reckon to have grown closest to Christ have known, like John of the Cross, an agonizing night of the soul, or, like Mother Teresa, long times of gnawing doubt and inner purposelessness.

The gospel, however, would hardly be good news if this were its only, or its last word on death. And one thing that believers and non-believers alike are pretty clear about is that Christian faith offers hope in the face of death. They differ, of course, as to whether there is any reliability or truth in that hope. And here it is that, once again, a Christian account of hope needs to take imperfection very seriously.

The trouble is this: just as our imagination can foster nightmares, so it can weave dreams and illusions. And nowhere will it be more tempted to work at weaving them than in the face of death. Some people may think this is what faith is really meant to do: to build castles of fantasy in the air and then to long so fervently for them to be real that we *will* them into some kind of enduring reality. If people do think like this, it may not help matters that funeral services are among the most frequent occasions for non-churchgoers to encounter preachers. Those of us who preach on such occasions are more than likely to be asked by relatives of the deceased to read out, or listen to, the text that begins with the shocking words, 'Death is nothing at all.' Poor Henry Scott Holland, the author of the words, would be appalled to know how they have been torn from their original context, in a sermon he preached at St Paul's Cathedral after the death of King Edward VII.[4] The sermon, entitled 'The King of Terrors', of which the passage we hear at funerals is a small part, does not end up saying that death is nothing. In fact it explores two contradictory or paradoxical aspects of our experience of death: our feeling of its brutality and cruelty ('It is the cruel ambush into which we are snared. It is the pit of destruction. It wrecks, it defeats, it shatters.') and the quite contradictory inner conviction of personal continuity through death. Faith, according to Scott Holland, has to make sense of *both* these aspects of experience. Sadly, but quite understandably, at the point of grief we are tempted to focus only on the soothing message of continuity. But if that is all that is offered by the preacher, a sweet but insubstantial dream has been substituted for the gospel.

Our limitedness in the face of death is insurmountable. At this point we are well and truly outside Eden, seeing, if we see at all, 'through a glass, darkly'. There is no exempted category of human beings – whether spiritual mediums, scientists or saints – who are given sight of what lies beyond the grave. Priests and ministers certainly have no second sight. Because Christian faith is such a real, robust source of courage and hope in the presence of death, it is easy to slip into thinking of it as a kind of 'knowing' that bypasses normal human limitation and imperfection. But it is not. Faith, when we face death, is precisely God's gift to the unknowing, the ignorant. It may be a gift of comfort, yes, but neither aiming, nor able, simply to soothe. Here we can see why faith does not endorse our dreams and fantasies, and here – above all – we can see how God's grace does not displace human imperfection but works with it.

In each chapter of this book the same theme has emerged in different ways: the theme that the gospel is about God not fulfilling our dreams, but fulfilling something more real, more mysterious and ultimately surely even more wonderful. In every previous instance, thinking about the messes we get into in our lives, our church, or our prayers, I have been able to write from experience, sometimes to give examples. When it comes to discussing death, experience is precisely what we don't have. So we can only explore the meaning of faith at the very limit of life by returning to the source and foundation of faith. We have to look beyond our dreams.

I know what is desirable, in the face of death. It would be desirable, more desirable than I can put into words, for there to be a way of continuing to live beyond death, a way that allowed me still to be 'me', yet without the damage I do, the pain I feel and the tears I shed. Just as importantly, it would be desirable for those who mean everything to me here to be with me there. It would be good, too, if there were to be something like the adorable *particularity* that makes the universe I now live in so entrancing, some kind of equivalent to colour, density, sound, smell. All this, of course, would need to be suffused with the light and love of God, otherwise it would not be heaven and it could not endure eternally.

There is nothing in the Christian faith, or in the New Testament, that makes that kind of dream impossible. Countless believers, I suspect, hold to something like that dream or longing. If there is anything wrong with it, it is not the fact that it cannot be tested or proven: the same is true of many valuable beliefs. What is wrong with it is all to do with this: it distorts the very nature of faith. In this longing the wings of faith are made to carry *my* wishes to heaven. But faith is not there to wing my wishes to God, to serve as a vehicle for wish-fulfilment. Not that God is uninterested in my longings – Jesus told us to be quite outspoken about them when we pray. But prayer does not turn my desires into articles of faith. The wings of faith have quite another purpose: they are given to carry to me the genuine hope that comes from God.

The desire of the first disciples was that Jesus would go on and on. They almost certainly dreamed and spoke of a heavenly destination at the end of the earthly ministry they shared with him. They discussed who would have pride of place on the day of their vindication. They surely had more justification for dreaming of exultation than many of us. They had left their boats, their trades, their homes and their families to follow him. But the dream was extinguished. There was no path to heaven that led by the route of their desires. Instead, Jesus was handed over to death, humiliated, crucified and buried. 'We had hoped', in the words of two disappointed disciples, reported by Luke, 'that he was the one to redeem Israel' (Luke 24.21).

The fracture of their hope remains. The resurrection of Jesus does not reinstate that first dream of theirs. When Christ did rise from the dead, everything about their encounters with him makes it clear that they had no idea that it would be like this. Once having encountered the reality of life from the dead, they must have been mortally embarrassed about their former hopes and ambitions. And now they are no longer interested in the question of who sits where at the heavenly banquet. Now it seems that they are at once reduced and enlarged by what they have witnessed. Their trust and confidence are enlarged as they begin to stand up and proclaim the message of life and hope in Jesus' name; their self-concern shrinks as they share food and property with each other.

The discovery of the empty tomb and the appearances of Jesus in his risen life are events of terror and wonder. In these events the disciples find themselves judged, forgiven, transfixed and commissioned for service. The result has little to do with comfortable and comforting fantasies. Dreams of what our imagination counts as paradise are replaced with a humbling, cleansing and energizing hope.

The only message about life beyond death that Christians are authorized to proclaim is the message that emerges from these events and from the words of the crucified and risen Jesus. It is through this lens – Christ's death and resurrection – that we are to look at death and to seek hope beyond death. The message we are given, then, is deeply trustful but also deeply agnostic. In Christ we see that God is to be trusted with our lives, as we live them and as we lose them. No manner or kind of death puts us out of the reach of the loving power of God to raise. Nor do we die alone, separated from the community of faith. As Kenneth Wilson puts it: 'we die still surrounded by [the] company of faithful witnesses, and therefore also in the presence of Christ'.[5]

But if we want to know what being raised by God might look like, or when to expect it, we are resolutely refused an answer. Instead, like the first disciples at the scene of Christ's ascension, we are told not to keep staring up to heaven. Better spend our time, whatever our age, learning how to live.

It is in the light of the ending of the Gospels, with Jesus' death and resurrection, that we begin to get a better grasp of something Jesus said earlier:

> If any want to become my followers, let them deny themselves and take up their cross and follow me. For those who want to save their life will lose it, and those who lose their life for my sake, and for the sake of the gospel, will save it. (Mark 8.34–35)

It proves that his dying is the most dramatic and compelling summary of how we are invited to live. We are meant to live as people who give away – perhaps more carelessly, lose – our lives: not as people who try to deny their limitations and inadequacies or to hang on to their lives both for now and for eternity, but as those who let go in trust.

The poet David Scott, writing of Easter, puts himself in the place of the women at the end of Mark's Gospel who see the empty tomb and run away, afraid (Mark 16.8):

> I am with the women
> falling off the end of the gospel
> afraid. This year I may learn to fall
> and not fear, and find myself lifted
> to watch the face of forgiveness rise
> with such silence and uncanny grace . . .[6]

'To fall and not fear, and find myself lifted'; captured here in a few words is that large aspect of the gospel that is trampoline-like and centred on trust. People who have lived in trust with God for many years often show two special facets: a perpetual gleam of humour, as if they glimpse an element of comedy – the comedy of a passing pageant – in everything around them, and a sense of tranquillity about death.

The resurrection of Jesus has always been, to my understanding, the firmest foundation for faith in eternal life. But next to that has been the experience of seeing people who have lived in trust and who die in serenity – and here serenity means something more than contentment. It means a quality that generates its own unique atmosphere, palpable in the room (as other witnesses will tell you). I first knew this watching with a dying woman, in bed in the front room of a house in Sunderland, 20 years ago. We had been together in that room for a few days, and this was the last. The room returns to me again now, and I think of it as the most peaceful place I have ever known. Again David Scott has put his finger on it:

> The light that emanated from the space
> she left spoke resurrection.[7]

Ignorant as we are, we cannot say whether human imperfection is taken away at this point. We can only say that it no longer seems to matter.

In the end, I suspect that the great novelist William Golding had got it right when he wrote of his conviction 'that both comedy and tragedy outside books as well as in them are subsumed in an ultimate Dazzle'.[8] And perhaps the dying words of Victor Hugo, the novelist, point the same way: 'I see black light.'

Notes

Introduction: well outside Eden

1 Quoted in Peter Ackroyd, *Blake* (London: Sinclair-Stevenson, 1995), p. 67.
2 W. H. Auden, *Collected Poems*, ed. Edward Mendelson (London: Faber and Faber Ltd, 2007, and used by permission). An excellent survey of his faith and its influence on his writing is presented in Arthur Kirsch, *Auden and Christianity* (New Haven and London: Yale University Press, 2005).
3 Number IX of *Twelve Songs*, dated April 1936, in *Collected Poems*, p. 141.

1 Recognizing where we are: facing up to imperfection

1 In November 1937, according to *Collected Poems* (London: Faber and Faber Ltd, 2007), p. 135.
2 Some would argue rather the opposite: Rowan Williams, in 'Reflections on Art and Love', *Grace and Necessity* (London: Continuum, 2005, p. 21), refers to the Catholic philosopher Jacques Maritain's view 'of the finite beauty and finishedness of the work [of art] being always incomplete at some level, "limping" like the biblical Jacob; achieved art always has "*that kind* of imperfection through which infinity wounds the finite".'
3 These words used here are a paraphrase.
4 This phrase is used by Charles Wesley to describe the wounds in the hands and side of the risen Christ in his great Advent hymn, 'Lo! He comes with clouds descending'.
5 Arthur Kirsch, *Auden and Christianity* (New Haven and London: Yale University Press, 2005), p. 173, quotes Auden as remarking to his secretary and friend, Alan Ansen, that 'sexual fidelity is more important in a homosexual relationship than in any other. In other relationships there are a variety of ties. But here, fidelity is the only bond.'

2 Loving our mess: the gospel and human unsuccess

1 Nicola Slee, *The Book of Mary* (London: SPCK, 2007), 'Visitation, Chartres'. Reproduced by permission.
2 Maynard Solomon, *Mozart: A Life* (London: Random House, 1995), p. 205.
3 Broadcast on ITV on Sunday 25 May 2008.

4 Thomas Harris, *I'm OK, You're OK* (New York: Harper and Row, 1967).

5 Ernest Kurtz and Katherine Ketcham, *The Spirituality of Imperfection: Storytelling and the Search for Meaning* (New York: Random House, 1992), pp. 28 and 47.

6 Rowan Williams, *Silence and Honey Cakes: The Wisdom of the Desert* (Oxford: Lion, 2003), p. 89.

7 James Alison, *Living in the End Times* (London: SPCK, 1997), p. 167.

8 David Hare, *Racing Demon* (London: Faber and Faber Ltd, 1990, and used by permission).

9 W. H. Vanstone, *Love's Endeavour, Love's Expense: The Response of Being to the Love of God* (London: Darton, Longman and Todd, 1977), p. 47.

3 Unlimited company: the glimpse of a Holy Communion

1 The description is given in an article Auden wrote for the *New York Times*, 'Two sides of a thorny problem' (1 March 1953, section 2), where the experience is ascribed to someone else, but it seems clear that he is describing the incident that occurred to him in the early 1930s. Cited in Arthur Kirsch, *Auden and Christianity* (New Haven and London: Yale University Press, 2005), pp. 12–13.

2 'A Summer Night', *Collected Poems*, ed. Edward Mendelson (London: Faber and Faber Ltd, 2007, and used by permission), p. 117, written in June 1933.

3 *The Church of the Triune God*, The Cyprus Agreed Statement of the International Commission for Anglican–Orthodox Theological Dialogue (London: Anglican Communion Office, 2007), p. 15.

4 Nicholas M. Healy, *Church, World and the Christian Life* (Cambridge: Cambridge University Press, 2000), outlines a persuasive critique of 'blueprint ecclesiologies' giving particular attention to 'Communion' ecclesiology.

5 The title of a book by John A. T. Robinson, written towards the end of his life, primarily concerned with the relation of Christianity and Buddhism: *The Truth is Two-Eyed* (London: SCM Press, 1979).

6 This expression, now widely used in ecumenical theology, was coined by de Lubac (1896–1991) in his ground-breaking book *Corpus Mysticum* (1944).

7 Kirsch, *Auden and Christianity*, p. 3.

8 Rowan Williams, in his essay on Michael Ramsey in *Anglican Identities* (London: Darton, Longman and Todd, 2004), p. 88.

9 Michael Ramsey, *The Gospel and the Catholic Church* (London: Longmans, Green & Co., 1936, 1956; new edition SPCK, 1990).

10 Ramsey, *The Gospel and the Catholic Church* (1956), p. 220.

4 Dazzling darkness: God and silence, knowing and ignorance

1 W. H. Auden, *Modern Canterbury Pilgrims*, quoted in Arthur Kirsch, *Auden and Christianity* (New Haven and London: Yale University Press, 2005), p. 22.

2 The perceptive comment of John Fuller in *W. H. Auden: A Commentary* (London: Faber and Faber Ltd, 1998), p. 461.

3 T. S. Eliot, 'East Coker', part III, from *Four Quartets* in *Collected Poems* (London: Faber and Faber Ltd, 1974, and used by permission), p. 200.

4 Eliot, 'East Coker', in *Collected Poems*, p. 201, used by permission.

5 Gerard Manley Hopkins, 'God's Grandeur'.

6 Words from St Augustine, which John Henry Newman took as his motto.

7 W. H. Auden, 'A Thanksgiving', *Collected Poems*, ed. Edward Mendelson (London: Faber and Faber Ltd, 2007, and used by permission), p. 890, probably written in May 1973.

8 Lyndall Gordon, *T. S. Eliot: An Imperfect Life* (London: Vintage, 1998), p. 133. Lyndall Gordon's study of Eliot's life and poetry sheds particular light on the influence of his religious background, and later commitment to the Church, on the genesis of his poetry.

9 T. S. Eliot, 'Little Gidding', parts II and IV, from *Four Quartets* in *Collected Poems*, pp. 219 and 221, used by permission. See also Lyndall Gordon's commentary on 'Little Gidding' in *T. S. Eliot*, pp. 369–87.

10 Eliot, 'Little Gidding', part IV, from *Four Quartets* in *Collected Poems*, p. 221.

11 Augustine, *Confessions*, book 1, chapter 1, part 1.

12 Jeremy Taylor, *Holy Living, Holy Dying*.

13 Julian of Norwich, *Revelations of Divine Love* (London: Penguin, 1966), p. 183.

14 Simone Weil, *Gravity and Grace* (London: Routledge, 1947/2002), p. 120.

15 Ascribed to John Bunyan in 'Mr Bunyan's Dying Sayings' published in Offor's 1861 edition of *Bunyan's Works*.

16 Thomas Traherne, *Centuries*, III, part 1. Traherne lived from 1637 to 1674, although most of his writings, including *Centuries*, were not published under his name until the twentieth century. Here I quote from *Thomas Traherne: Poems, Centuries and Three Thanksgivings*, ed. Anne Ridler (London: Oxford University Press, 1966), p. 263.

17 Anselm's phrase, which is the best short description of Christian theology.

18 Henry Vaughan, 'The Night'.

5 Salt of the earth: what kind of difference are we meant to make?

1 W. H. Auden, 'Writing', from *Selected Essays* (London: Faber and Faber Ltd, 1964), p. 27.
2 W. H. Auden, 'Many Happy Returns (for John Rettger)', in *Collected Poems*, ed. Edward Mendelson (London: Faber and Faber Ltd, 2007, and used by permission), p. 320.
3 Auden, 'Mundus et Infans', *Collected Poems*, p. 325.
4 Auden, 'Writing', in *Selected Essays*, p. 38.
5 Auden, 'In Memory of W. B. Yeats', *Collected Poems*, p. 248.
6 Karl Kraus, quoted in W. H. Auden, *Secondary Worlds* (London: Faber and Faber Ltd, 1969), p. 22.
7 In his poem of 1969, 'Epistle to a Godson (for Philip Spender)', Auden represents his choice of subject matter for poetry 'the small ... wonders of Nature and of households', and his chosen poetic tone – 'a serio-comic note' – as the right and necessary means to give nourishment to a younger generation facing a 'brave new world' with its threat of annihilation.
8 Gutiérrez died on 23 February 2008; quotations are from his obituary in *The Times*, 19 March 2008.
9 John Keats in a letter to George and Thomas Keats, 22 December 1817.
10 Auden, *For the Time Being, Complete Poems*, p. 391, used by permission.
11 Auden, *For the Time Being, Complete Poems*, p. 394, used by permission.
12 Gillian Rose, *Mourning Becomes the Law* (Cambridge: Cambridge University Press, 1996). See particularly her discussion of representations of the Holocaust and of Fascism in books and films, pp. 41–54.
13 Charles Handy, *Myself and Other More Important Matters* (London: Arrow Books, 2007), pp. 35ff.
14 Rowan Williams, *Silence and Honey Cakes: The Wisdom of the Desert* (Oxford: Lion, 2003).
15 Handy, *Myself and Other More Important Matters*, p. 37.

6 Imperfect evangelism: treasure in clay pots

1 David Hare, *Racing Demon* (London: Faber and Faber Ltd, 1990, used by permission), p. 66.
2 Quoted in William Hague, *William Wilberforce* (London: HarperPress, 2007), p. 209.
3 Hague, *William Wilberforce*, p. 502.
4 Gillian Rose, *Love's Work* (London: Chatto and Windus, 1995).
5 Rose, *Love's Work*, p. 98.
6 Rose, *Love's Work*, pp. 6f.
7 Rose, *Love's Work*, p. 6.

8 C. K. Barrett, *The Second Epistle of Paul to the Corinthians* (London: A & C Black, 1973), p. 133.

9 Alan Bennett, *Talking Heads* (London: BBC Books, 1988), p. 31. Although there are anachronistic touches in the caricature of Anglican church life that Bennett paints in 'Bed Among the Lentils', it is so mercilessly, comically acute that the reader (as so often with his writing) doesn't know whether to laugh or cry.

7 The shadow of death and the light of grace

1 Karl Barth, *Church Dogmatics*, III/2 (Edinburgh: T&T Clark, 1960), p. 597.

2 Quoted by Humphrey Carpenter, *W. H. Auden: A Biography* (Boston: Houghton Mifflin, 1981), p. 317.

3 Keats' sonnet, 'When I have fears that I may cease to be', sent in a letter to J. H. Reynolds in January 1818, three years before his death, and published posthumously.

4 The theology of the sermon is analysed in an article by John Heidt, 'The King of Terrors: The Theology of Henry Scott Holland'. *Contemporary Review*, March 2000.

5 Kenneth Wilson, *Dying to Live: A Christian Approach to the Matter of Mortality* (Peterborough: Epworth Press, 2008), p. 107.

6 David Scott, 'Easter (I)' in *Piecing Together* (Northumberland: Bloodaxe Books, 2005), p. 60. Reproduced by permission.

7 David Scott, 'Resurrection' in *Piecing Together*, p. 63. Reproduced by permission.

8 William Golding, *To the Ends of the Earth* (London: Faber and Faber Ltd, 1991), p. xi.

Index

Abraham 31–2
absolution 85; *see also* confession
acceptance 16–19; *see also* gospel
addiction 17, 18, 61
Alan of Lille 54
Alison, James 23
Auden, W. H.: and Chester Kallman
  72, 78; 'Christmas Oratorio' *For
  the Time Being* 7, 78–9; faith xiv,
  2, 29–30, 46; Herod, as depicted
  by 78–9; homosexuality 7; love
  of life 99–100; and Marxism 72;
  poem 'Epistle to a Godson' 109
  n5.7; poem 'In Memory of W. B.
  Yeats' 69, 71; poem 'In Sickness
  and in Health' 10–11, 40, 74;
  poem 'Progress' 100; poem
  'Talking to Myself' 99; poems
  Horae Canonicae 47; on poetry
  69–72; *The Rake's Progress* 72, 78;
  and Stravinsky 72, 78; and the
  Spanish Civil War 72; and war 46,
  59

Baldwin, Stanley 77
baptism 35, 38, 39
Barrett, C. K. 94–5
Barth, Karl 99
beauty 4–5
Bennett, Alan 96
Biko, Steve 97
Blair, Tony 75
Blake, William xiii
body, attitudes to 48–50
Book of Common Prayer 14, 37,
  41
born-again Christians 91–2
Bunyan, John 64

certainty 77
chaos 11, 12, 13
Church: as a communion 29–45;
  as historical community 35–40
Church of England 37, 57–8
churches, imperfections of 32–3
clergy 89, 91
commitment 57–9, 73
communion (Eucharist) 36–7
communion (*koinonia*) 29–45
confession 26–7, 85–6
conversion 91–2; of Paul 95
Corinthians, Paul's letters to the
  94–5
Cromwell, Oliver 74
cross, way of the 87
crucifix 87
Crystal Palace 81

Damascus road 95
death 99–105; faith and hope in face
  of 101, 103
dispossession 50–1, 55, 58, 60
diversity 40–4
doubt 100, 101
dreams 79–84, 101–4

Edna (cancer survivor) 93
ekklesia 31
Eliot, T. S. 46–8; marriages 59–60;
  poem 'East Coker' 50; poem 'Little
  Gidding' 60
embarrassment 43–4, 51–2, 87, 90,
  95
empty tomb 104, 105
environment 50
Eucharist 36–7
evangelism 89–98

111